EDITED BY KIRSTEN IRVING

WITH A FOREWORD BY

OPERA 3
FULMINARE'S REVENGE

& JON STONE

KIERON GILLEN

SIDEKICK BOOKS

www.drfulminare.com

First published in 2013 by

SIDEKICK BOOKS

Printed by
Lavenham Press Ltd
47 Water Street
Lavenham CO10 9RN

Typeset in Pixelmix and Wonder Boy in Monster World
Sidekick Books logo font: Roman Antique

'Black Cover' by Jon Stone
'White Cover' by Mike Stone

Special thanks to Seb Manley and Julia Scheib.

"Well, looks like another trip to the mortuary ..."

~

ISBN: 978-0-9564164-7-6

CONTENTS

Foreword by KIERON GILLEN ━ ———————— 9
Introduction by JON STONE ～～～～～～→ 11

STAGE 1: DUST-UP FOREST

KAYO CHINGONYI
Fist of the North Star ● · · · · · · · · · · · · · · · · · · · 19
SAMUEL PRINCE
Target: Renegade ◖ · 20
ROSS SUTHERLAND
Ryu · · ♥ 21
Ken ◖ · 22
Blanka ～～～～～～～～～～～～～～→ 23
JON STONE
How Weak You Are! ● · · · · · · · · · · · · · · · · · · 24
MATT HAIGH
The Thirteenth Colossus · · · · · ♥ · · · · · · · · · 32
JOE DUNTHORNE
The Fates Attend a Robert McKee Seminar · · · · 34
NATHAN PENLINGTON
Tekken Love Poem ◖ · · · · · · · · · · · · · · · · · · · 36
PHIL BROWN
Side Scroller ━ ——— ——— ——— 37
ALIYA WHITELEY
Groan ◖ · 38
DAVID FLOYD
Daley Thompson plays *Daley Thompson's Supertest*
on a ZX Spectrum emulator · · · · · · · · · 🍒 · · · · · · · 40
SIMON BARRACLOUGH
Soldier of Fortune ⚔ - - - - - - - - - - - - - - 42
RICHARD WATT
Pit Boss · · · · · ♥ · 43

S.J. FOWLER
Golden Axe ···························· 44
KIRSTEN IRVING & ABIGAIL PARRY
Multi-player Versus Poems ~~~~~~~~~~→ 45

END OF LEVEL BOSS
Women Who Fight ························· 48

STAGE 2: PLUCK & PLUNDER ISLAND

MELISSA LEE-HOUGHTON
Hot Pursuit ·························· 58
JON STONE
Caligula Prepares to Join the Party ·········· 64
E. KRISTIN ANDERSON
The Independent Contractor ············· 67
That Metroid Guy is a Lady ··············· 68
CHARLOTTE GEATER
Dragon Theories ······················ 69
BEN WILKINSON
Link's Awakening ← ← ← ← ← ← ← 70
NIALL CAMPBELL
The Player Lost in Ganon's Tower ··········· 71
CHRISSY WILLIAMS
Listening to Midna ······················ 72
Robot Unicorn Attack ···················· 74
Mirror, Okami, Stardust ·············· 75
JOE DUNTHORNE
Dear Jaffar, ← —— —— —— —— —— 76
PHIL BROWN
Sonic Senryu ······················ 77
S.J. FOWLER
Altered Beast ························· 78
Donkey Kong ✻ ✻ ✻ ✻ ✻ ✻ ✻ ✻ 79

RICHARD WATT
Dragon's Lair ·· ♥ ······························ 80
ROSS SUTHERLAND
Gauntlet 〔····································· 82
SAM BUCHAN-WATTS
The October Revolution
and a Golden Chocobo ◄— —————— ——— 86
CLAIRE TREVIEN
Past Simple 〔··································· 88
CHELSEA CARGILL
Manic Miner, 48 Kilobytes ·····♥·············· 89
Sabre Wulf, circa 1984 〔······················ 90
Valhalla 〔···································· 91
GABRIELLE NOLAN
Ico ·· ♥······························· 92
HARRIET MOORE
Dreams of a House ◄ ❀ ❀ ❀ ❀ ❀ ❀ ❀ ❀ 94
KIRSTEN IRVING
Arcadia ········ ⸎····················· 96
KATE POTTS
Doomdark's Revenge 〔···················· 98
MATT HAIGH & JOHN CLEGG
Multi-player Party Gathering Poems ⸙〜〜〜➔ 100

END OF LEVEL BOSS
Cento for a Nameless One 〔················ 104

STAGE 3: BRAINTHUNDER MOUNTAIN

CHARLOTTE RUNCIE
In My Pocket 〔························· 112
ISOBEL DIXON
Pinball Electra ⸙ ← ← ← ← ← ← ← ← 113

KIRSTEN IRVING
Pinball Dreams 114
Ten Green Bottles 116
CLIFF HAMMETT
Snake 118
CHRISSY WILLIAMS
Sonnet for Zookeeper 119
HOLLY HOPKINS
Samorost 120
LUKE KENNARD
Spaceships with Guns Bigger Than
The Spaceships Themselves   122
Partial Inheritance 124
SIMON BARRACLOUGH
Piggle Peggle 125
EMILY HASLER
Objection! 126
BEN STAINTON
Fingers on Pause 128
MM 129
POSIE RIDER
The Sims 130
DAN SIMPSON
Sympathy for the Orange Ghost 132
FRANCINE RUBIN
The World Is Tetris 134
JAMES BROOKES
Dia de Muertos 1998 136
HARRY MAN
Lines Derived From
Minecraft Player Queries 137
EMILY HASLER & JOHN CANFIELD
Multi-player Strategy Poems 138

END OF LEVEL BOSS
Headstone Fortress 142

(Return of the) Introduction 🎮 · · · · · · · · · · · · · · · · · 152

Index by Game Title   · · · · · ● · · · · · · · · · · · · · · · · · · · 154
Notes and Cheats   🍒 · 156
Contributor Notes   👾 ✦ ✦ ✦ ✦ ✦ ✦ ✦ ✦ ✦ 159

ACKNOWLEDGEMENTS

'Fist of the North Star' by Kayo Chingonyi was first published in *Some Bright Elegance* (Salt Publishing, 2012).

'Ryu', 'Ken' and 'Blanka' by Ross Sutherland were first published in *Hyakuretsu Kyaku* (Penned in the Margins, 2011).

'Tekken Love Poem' was first published in *Almost Nearly* (Shortfuse, 2008).

'Soldier of Fortune' by Simon Barraclough was first published in *Neptune Blue* (Salt Publishing, 2011).

'Robot Unicorn Attack' by Chrissy Williams was first published in *Flying Into The Bear* (Happenstance, 2013).

'In My Pocket' by Charlotte Runcie was first published in *The Salt Book of Younger Poets* (Salt Publishing, 2011).

'Pinball Dreams' by Kirsten Irving was first published in *Never Never Never Come Back* (Salt Publishing, 2012).

FOREWORD

I'M feeling somewhat extraneous. In his introductory essay, Editor Stone explores the meaningful comparisons you can make between two forms that appear radically different. But first I'm going to blather confessionally. Bear with me. Or don't – you can skip to the poems, obviously. I won't hold it against you.

I have written two sets of poems about video games.

One was actually arguably my first review. It was about *Defender* and shamelessly ripped off the structure of Big Phil Larkin's 'As Bad as a Mile'. It was called '49,000', and described a tragic *Defender* game that ended when my final life was lost just 100 points – a single alien, a single shot – before I managed to secure an extra life. Clearly a traumatic event in my teenage life, well worth immortalising in verse.

My second was a series of found poems in which I rearranged the argumentative trash-talk of the powerfully be-thighed Chun-Li into lovelorn emo poetry. I seem to remember at least one funny line, though equally seem to be unable to recall what it was, which casts some doubts on that first assertion.

The more serious poems herein are infinitely better than the former; the more humorous poems are infinitely better than the latter. Best of all, many are both simultaneously, which is the world-view whose corner I'm always willing to stand in, grasping a towel and ready to cut the bruises above the eye if things get rough.

Fundamentally, I like this volume so much, I'm willing to forgive Ross Sutherland for writing about bloody Ryu.

KIERON GILLEN

INTRODUCTION

COMMANDER, thank goodness you're here! That is, I assume you're the Commander. This is kind of a one-way signal – all I've got here is a life-sign on my screen. No audio, no visual. But you're here, and that's good enough. Once you've put on your hazard suit, kindly proceed through the airlock.

I don't know how thoroughly you've been briefed on the *Coin Opera 2* project thus far, so let me run you through the basics. The first *Coin Opera* was a tentative experiment, aiming to combat two prejudices simultaneously: the prejudice against computer games that denies the artistry of their content, and the prejudice against contemporary poetry that rejects its readability and relevance. Games can, of course, be crude and violent, while poetry can be dry and pompous, but there is much more to both than meets the cynical eye, and the results of *Coin Opera* led us to believe that the two mediums have much to say to each other. Hence *Coin Opera 2: Fulminare's Revenge.*

Hm, that's strange. I don't seem to have a file for you, Commander. I hope you *are* the Commander! Of course you are. Anyway, without a file, I can't assume your familiarity with either poetry or gaming. I'll try to give you the briefest of run-downs, just in case you find yourself insufficiently armed.

If you're generally comfortable with poetry, then the content of games, even at its most alien, only represents an iteration of the 'Otherworld' that poets have returned to throughout the ages, from Ovid's bibling of tales of transformation and divine intervention, through Yeats' Irish folklore (*"Faeries, come take me out of this dull world / For I would ride with you upon the wind!"*) and Coleridge's drug-induced vision of Kubla Kahn, to the dark universe of Ted Hughes' *Crow*. Games suggest a thousand variations on Prospero's island. Throughout the 80s and 90s, they were mainly inhabited by sprites, but they also contain their fair share of daemons, gods, therianthropes, mythic heroes and so on. They are rich sources of symbolism and parable, steeped in their own lore and ripe for literary exploration.

If you suspect you are inadequately prepared for poetry, the main thing to remember is that poems resist the stipulation that exists in other written mediums to convey a straightforward message – not as a test of your intelligence, but in order to give primacy to their qualities of weight and structure, music and mood. They are a kind of architecture or sound engineering, each finely tuned little machine singing with individual purpose. Good poems have a long half-life; their immediate effect is subtle, even uncertain, but they reveal more of themselves over time and bear out multiple revisits. They are curiously-shaped keys to locks we are only dimly aware of.

Proceed into the atrium when you're ready, Commander. Please watch your step – the *Coin Opera 2* project developed in ways we didn't initially anticipate. It became clear to us, for example, that the two mediums have a lot more in common than we thought. Consider:

1) Resistance. You don't expect to be able to run through a computer game from start to finish without encountering any obstacles. Overcoming those obstacles is where the real engagement lies. The player has to recognise themselves as an agent, not a passive observer. Poetry operates on a similar principle. It's the way the mind snags on, and is held up by, carefully deployed sounds and patterns, by ambiguities and elusiveness, that lends an effective poem much of its sense of artistry and control. When either a poem or a game is finished too easily, when there is nothing left to collect or resolve, it loses most of its potency and allure.

2) Formal restriction. Though it's less true of gaming in recent years, computer games of the 70s, 80s and 90s were characterised by the limitations of their technology. A programmer for a ZX Spectrum would have to cram code, graphics and sound effects onto a spool of audio tape, while depth of field, prior to polygons, was created chiefly through various kinds of illusion. Though the restrictions may be less apparent now, games remain a medium in which overcoming logistical problems is a major creative component, something that connects them to the traditions of formal structure in poetry.

Poets create similar conditions artificially, choosing structural rules by which they must abide. This is done both to achieve a pleasing aesthetic and to inspire solutions to the problems inevitably presented. Some game developers now deliberately work with older systems or imitate past graphical limitations for the same reasons.

It's also interesting to note how formal impositions can be expressed through the level architecture of a game. *Sonic the Hedgehog 2*'s 'zones' are arranged like stanzas with Dr Robotnik's appearance as a repeating end-line and the final two bosses of the game as an envoi. And if modern games play more like free verse, they still rely heavily on rhythm and repetition.

2) Speed of change. Within poetry and gaming communities alike, old orders are being challenged by a generation empowered by new technologies. Young developers can now not only create games in their spare time, but can access a worldwide audience without endorsement from publishers (Daisuke 'Pixel' Amaya, creator of *Cave Story*, and Markus 'Notch' Persson, creator of *Minecraft*, are two examples). Poets, meanwhile, no longer require a major prize win to garner an audience but publish independently and collaboratively online.

In both fields, this has resulted in a shake-up to predominantly conservative mentalities – the infatuation with fantasy heroics in gaming, and with plodding personal anecdotalage in poetry.

4) Play. Commander, this might seem all too obvious, but its importance mustn't be underestimated. Play is one way of continually testing and adjusting the boundaries of culture, or conversely, through the apparatus of rules and goals, reinforcing certain ideals and models of behaviour. This is true of games both before and after the invention of the microprocessor. One only has to look at *Monopoly*, 'the rage of America' in 1936, and its subversion in Professor Ralph Anspach's *Anti-Monopoly*, a direct response to the 'lessons' taught by the original game. In Benjamin Franklin's 'On the Morality of Chess', he asserts that chess is 'not merely an idle amusement', but also teaches foresight, circumspection, caution and hope.

The surrealists understood all too well what this means for art. They recognised the potential in any system of rules for exploration of the subconscious, and notable works drew on the architecture of board games – Giacometti's *Circuit* and *On ne joue plus*, for example. Many of today's virtual worlds seem to answer arch-surrealist André Breton's call to arms, so much so that it seems spookily prescient:

> *I believe in the future resolution of the states of dream and reality – in appearance so contradictory – in a sort of absolute reality, or surréalité.*

Games are systems in which we 'play', and poets too are engaged in a kind of play, testing what is possible within the rule-set of language, rearranging the world a morsel at a time, obeying and disobeying arbitrary stipulations. The philosopher Bernard Suits described gaming as 'the voluntary attempt to overcome unnecessary obstacles', which could just as easily apply to the writing of a sonnet.

You have doubts, Commander? Are you thinking that players of games have an active role in the games they play, whereas readers of poems only experience that 'game' passively, as spectators? It's not quite as binary as that. Many games (most notoriously *Dragon's Lair*) enrol the player in a predetermined course of events, requiring only occasional button presses or repetitive procedures to make sure the story doesn't end prematurely. At the other end of the scale, a new wave of hyperliterature is testing how readers can be involved in shaping poems through online interaction, and as far back as 1961, Raymond Queneau invited user participation through his *Cent mille milliards de poèmes* project. It's deeper than that though – all poems require the reader to bring the toolkit of their own experience and imagination to make something of the words. Without the reader's mind, they're only markings on a page.

Commander, it's through this fourth point of commonality that *Coin Opera 2* chiefly exists. Both mediums excel in providing a safe space – what is called in gaming theory the 'magic circle' – in which risks can be taken and lines overstepped. The environment can be instantly reset if things go awry, and the player can begin again.

More than other forms of literature, poetry permits this through its brevity. Where fiction is burdened by the need to hold our attention across many chapters, and must do so using stabilising elements like identifiable characters and plot devices, the poet is liberated to experiment, fleetingly, with any idea or scenario, to collide languages and worlds. Not for nothing is 'playful' a popular descriptor on the back of poetry books. Poetry revels in its instability, making it a natural tool for interacting with the often irrational worlds of computer games, which are more easily negotiated through play than by the application of learning. Poetry can be an extension of the way we play computer games, a form of emergent gameplay. It can operate as a kind of hack that lets the poet meddle with the rules of the game, in the same way that level editors and source engines allow gamers to create 'mods' – new variations on the original game.

Take, for example, Posie Rider's invasion of the world of *The Sims*, a game in which the player's goal is to build a life and career for virtual suburbanites from the starting point of a spacious new property. Rider imbues the infantile dolls with a realistic froth of emotions, and in doing so injects them with an eerie self-awareness, suffusing the domestic setting of the game-world with shades of the uncanny : "we live / a thousand days without shifting or ageing."

Games are often set up to induce you to go beyond their apparent limits in order to succeed. 2011's *Terraria* dumps you in a procedurally generated landscape with little to no instruction, leaving you to find out for yourself what happens when you attack certain creatures, build a settlement or dig down through miles of mud and rock. Why stop, then, at what is permitted within the technical bounds of the game? Poems allow one to extend the playfield even further. Thus, in Harriet Moore's 'Dreams of a House', the day-night cycle and settlement-building of *Terraria* are taken as the starting point and the structural shell of the poem, but the world conjured up is quite distinct from that of the game. Luke Kennard's blurring of the imagery of *Wizkid* with shades of contemporary urban life ("A dog sits on the toilet reading why / The riots happened") might leave us wondering where the game world stops and ours begins. My co-editor Kirsten Irving, in 'Pinball Dreams', reimagines the architecture of a pinball table as an emotional debris field, removing the ball and scoreboard and placing the 'player' directly on the table.

Another recurring approach is to interpret the game-world as literally as possible and to explore the ensuing implications. So in Joe Dunthorne's 'Dear Jaffar,' the inevitable sex between the Prince of Persia and the princess he rescues must take into account their 'limited palette' and 'damnable / sprite collision'.

Ross Sutherland writes letters to the protagonists of *Gauntlet*, addressing their eternal captivity in the infinite loop of a dungeon quest, while Emily Hasler turns the step-by-step movement system of *Phoenix Wright: Ace Attorney* into a hyperreality of 'infinitely smaller actions', subtly referencing Zeno's paradoxes.

There are some appropriate – and surprising – links between form and level design as well. Phil Brown's choice of the senryu form when writing about *Sonic the Hedgehog* evokes the simplicity of 16-bit graphics and mimics, spatially, the repeating tiles of the stages. Simon Barraclough replicates a *Peggle* arena in a variation on concrete poetry, and Francine Rubin makes the notion of falling blocks integral to the shaping of her stanzas in 'The World Is Tetris'.

Roleplay, and the relationship between player and avatar, is the basis of comedy in David Floyd's 'Daley Thompson Plays *Daley Thompson's Supertest* on a ZX-Spectrum Emulator' and poignancy in Niall Campbell's 'The Player Lost in Ganon's Tower', while Chrissy Williams' 'Robot Unicorn Attack' works as a rhythmic adaptation of the eponymous browser game, translating the pulse of a player pressing 'Z' and 'X' into the driving meter of the poem.

These are my own interpretations, you understand, Commander. I've been engaging with them in much the same way I might engage with a room in *Portal*: trying to work out what to do with the components to hand. There is undoubtedly more than one solution and – Hell's bells, we've been breached! If I can just get to

TOO LATE!

THERE BEING AN ABSENCE OF PRINCESSES, I MUST INNOVATE! IF YOU WISH TO SEE MR STONE AGAIN, YOU WILL HAVE TO COMPLETE THE ENSUING STAGES! OR DO I MEAN PAGES?

STAGE ONE

DUST-UP FOREST

KAYO CHINGONYI
🔥
FIST OF THE NORTH STAR

A POUND, and I'm the man
with seven scars, true heir
to the school of Hokuto
Shinken, wandering the non-
descript badlands that always
mean world's end, lone hero,
the criminally insane mutated
to pale hulks, their bulbous heads
made flesh bombs, with the flick
of a wrist, so quick, it seems
I only stand still; win by an act
of will. This is a Hokuto master's
art: observe the foe's stopped heart,
intact, but for the dark spot where
the strike found its mark. I practised
first with melons. When they split
at the slightest touch, I called myself
a novice. When we cut them open
to see the fruit reduced to slush,
I became a student. When my finger-
tips moved as if full metal jackets,
I set off on the quest that is my life's
work. Chain-wielding bikers cannot
faze me. To face me is to invite death.

SAMUEL PRINCE
TARGET: RENEGADE

I strut superfly street-tough through trash-whipped precincts
assailed by death kittens in spiked chokers, mayhem leather,

You've not known pixelated pain until you've felt a bike chain
splendour your glutes, your abs affirmed by aluminium
baseball bat, dropkick or sucker punch.

necro-pimps in white *Moonwalker* tuxes with ferric canes,
steel-rimmed fedoras. A motorcycle symphony from alpha

You've not known revanchism until you've seen it exacted
in split-level car parks on faceless goons as the night
metastasizes into the strip-lit corners.

brute clones, the hostile yakking of foaming Mastiffs, past
the burnt-out chassis of muscle cars, the playground bums

You've not known electronica until it has soundtracked jab,
jab, roundhouse to a besuited Lurch in a private
members club – the penultimate pasting.

and punks liquor pickled, dukes up and coming on in a bare-
knuckle testudo of stonewashed denim and hoodlum beef.

You've not known fleshlust until you've met it in the stare
of steroid psychosis; a boss jacked on uppers, snorting
one final hit. Seems all Mr Bigs act like this.

ROSS SUTHERLAND

RYU

JAPAN, 150 lbs

¶¶ A student of Master Sheng Long, Ryu has developed into a pure warrior. Ryu has no home, no friends and no family. Instead, he wanders the globe seeking to test his skills against other fighters.

SNES MANUAL

From fairest heroes we desire a code
that locks our bare soles to the dojo floor;
Four kanji in blood, as was foretold
in chapter seven of *The Art of War.*
Crouch, Crouch Forward, Walk Forward, then Punch.
Electric Shotokan, push out your palms
And feel the cannonball of chi, the touch
of death that lives inside your arms.
Hadouken, he says, narrating the scene,
His mind filled with Master Sheng Long's retort:
How purity did not mean constantly
Hadoukening though every fight he fought.
Whoever fights like wind has but one blow;
One only fights themselves in different clothes.

KEN

USA, 169 lbs

The only other disciple of master Sheng Long, Ken is a natural athlete. Unfortunately, Ken's natural fighting skill has fuelled his giant ego. For the past year, Ken has let his skills deteriorate, spending most of his time making action films and lying on the beach with his girlfriend. Only a challenge from Ryu has rekindled his fighting spirit.

SNES MANUAL

RESET! OK, everyone, places please.
This time let's try it on the motorbike.
No, Ken, we need some close-ups. Then we'll see
what happened to your cappuccino. Lights!
Don't start the engine, Ken. Just look intense.
That's…yeah. Makeup, can we touch-up the scars?
Action. Cue fire. Don't look into the lens!
I know it's your life story, but some parts
will require the script. Next is the shot
where you decide to run off to LA.
Now, walk out on your father. Good. Now stop
right on your mark. Let's see a smile, and…hey…
your face…Ken, is this you trying to act?
Chair for Ken! Can we get one with a back?

BLANKA

BRAZIL, 218 lbs

Very little is known about this bizarre fighter from the jungles of Brazil. For years, the natives have reported seeing a half-man, half-beast roaming the rain forests. Using a technique he learnt from electric eels, Blanka can channel up to 1,000 volts through his skin. Anyone who tries to grab him during this time is in for a shocking discovery.

SNES MANUAL

THE CHILD held up his necklace, a rusty
nine-volt battery threaded through with wire.
Homem branco, he said, his other hand thrust
forward, in spasm, as if to summon fire.
Later, Maurice's fine white hair flew
straight up, like a column, as if he had
rubbed it against the balloon of the moon.
Oblivious, the old man just waved back.
At closing time, the tar sky turned to TV.
Men with rifles ran into the trees.
Later, their corpses showed signs of a beating,
yet not enough to cease their heartbeat.
They were earthed straight away. Back at the school
I watched their children pitch lightbulbs at the wall.

JON STONE

HOW WEAK YOU ARE!

IROHA

Y<small>OU DREAM</small> of the crane
who dreams herself human
to please you.
You have her undress,
pluck feather from her back.

ANDREW

In shot-sun scarlet,
gallant enters Japan.
He has no use
of a guide. Fixed to his rifle:
keenest compass needle.

YOSHITORA

Prince Hedgehog
whose quills are scabbards.
The girls faint:
his flurry is quick as pages
who are riffled by wind.

HOHMARU

Full of *sake*,
he can barely hold up
his glut of hair.
In the street, he stumbles into
threat of the whole world!

SUGOROKU

Plump pot
balanced on naked thighs.
What's in this,
vast-hearted funster?
Cannonade firework!

OCHA-MARO

All the things
become soul eventually.
The puppet-theatre
lifts his curtains to show you
feast of turning moons.

TAMTAM

Frog-nose mask,
topmost gurning god
of a totem.
You face into forest
when beasts near village.

JUBEI

Only one
spat-sharpened eye.
This all he needs
to sing your
strike to a stagger.

KUSAREGEDO

Sack-bellied giant
bangs the table, wants
boiled human,
cooked until flesh
lobster-red as his own.

KUROKO

Stagehand moves
into the foreground.
His face covered,
blank fan. His hands
begin strike semaphores.

UKYO

Plaguey lungs
make him bent as bough.
He make feathers
of tossed apples, poems.
Squall of precise stroke.

BASARA

Even tonight
the dead do *hojojutsu*.
This knot of man,
shawled by the nude ghost
of lover, chain to his guilt.

KYOSHIRO

Is this play
or is it the dance of death?
Stage effects:
spice of flame, flash blood.
Naginata reach your heart.

SHIZUMARU

Why do you carry
that umbrella with you?
"Well, you see,
I don't exactly remember.
But it keeps demon at bay."

HANZO

Paid jimmier
of heads from their posts.
Now gone again –
leaves blinding dust,
star in your cheek.

KUZUKI

One brother
rages like warning flag,
heart struck match.
He doesn't notice
blood's pepper taste.

SOGETSU

The other brother
heronishly cool,
a wave
gathering itself,
whose tip is knife.

ENJA

An imp, sprung
from volcano-jailhouse,
left in his wake
a path of cinders,
rich ash of all thing.

SUIJA

Some *kappa*
thirst to break banks
and bones,
more than anything
to mate like monsoon.

GENJURO

Your rival
is hungry. Done slaying,
he drinks.
Done drinking, he toss bowl,
empty, to bloody road.

CHARLOTTE

Huge metal eyelids
make the body strong.
But unhelmed,
her loosed hair glissades
when in lunge.

MINA

Blessed long-bow,
gentle swerve. Just like
her lonely trail,
her willow legs. Dance!
Little monster killer.

SIEGER

Red lion knight,
you are no Prince Albert
with your claw
like the fiddler crab's,
your molten ingot fist.

NAKORURU

Father Bull and you
from northern mountains,
to war on war.
Rain can punish the land
like hawk from the sky.

MATT HAIGH

THE THIRTEENTH COLOSSUS

D<small>ON'T</small> hate me for this – for my bloodied fists
caught up in your pelt's oasis,
thighs buried in stalactites of stubble,
scuffed by horns of bone like missiles.
My elbows and toes grapple
with your colossal, questing bulk, dappled
by strange growths. I grope for pulleys and ropes,
wicker and wood lodged in your spine;
grope in the colosseum of your head
sporting pillared teeth and smashed masonry.
The thrum and chug of you, liquid muscle
between my legs, twisted thickets of gristle,
the whir of engines, the heart's hydraulic pistons,
the accordion bellows of your cavernous lungs,
each blasted breath a mournful waltz – I feel it all.
Fossil of drowned worlds, fossil of the sky,
you twist ribbon-like between floating hills,
playful in your zigzagging as a box kite.
From this height I can taste everything:
the sea's cerulean blue hot as menthol,
the musk of your tough leatherette, old as earth.
I crawl over the crenulated battlements
of your body, flat on my belly, through
hessian tufts of tubers, frozen nodules;

across your mottled, granite-flecked hide
pocked with whiskers like sticks of gelignite.
Your back is a city whittled to ruin
and I the tourist who will infect and spoil you.
Don't hate me for the blade I slip into your sinew
then crack and twist as if disembowelling crayfish.
Every faucet of steaming black blood
splatters my cheeks, my tunic, my horned helmet –
and I know now how David felt, the spire of you
buckled, a brace of rabbits broken-necked,
as you descend from your former majesty,
the cloud fortress of each eye dispersing.

JOE DUNTHORNE

THE FATES ATTEND A ROBERT MCKEE SEMINAR

– WE OPEN on a cliff-top.

– Our man stands with his feet on the edge.

– We flashback to his wife and child – *murdered*…

– Murdered by who?

– It's a mystery.

– So *that's* why our man is so goddamn pumped!

– Seriously pumped. Halved. Gratuitously so.

– And seeking what? Revenge? Answers?

– Freedom from his nightmares!

– And so begins a journey.

– Marauded by foes.

– Set upon by minions.

– A trail of dismembered individuals.

– He seeks the person responsible.

– The *god* responsible…

– But no mortal can challenge a god.

– Unless…

– Unless the mortal is massive.

– Very, very large.

– A colossus. A man-mountain.

– Because he drank a potion?

– Or opened a box of some kind?

– A McGuffin.

34

– Bright knives of light from an elaborate box.

– Fiercely guarded and intricately carved.

– Guarded by what?

– A hydra…?

– Lava man?

– By hundreds of clones of our hero!

– Good grief!

– He opens the box.

– He becomes monumental.

– God versus mortal. Hand to hand.

– Destroying continents with each body slam.

– Who wins?

– Come on.

– Who wins?

– The Mortal wins, becoming capitalised, and demands
  his right to uninterrupted sleep!

– But the god says: 'Dream on'…

– Cue: waterfalls of blood.

– Still, our man is haunted by memories.

– So he decides to take his own life.

– And we're back at the cliff, falling fast.

NATHAN PENLINGTON
TEKKEN LOVE POEM

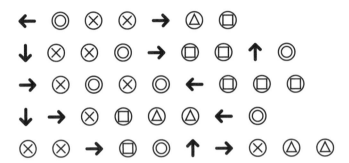

* To experience maximum expression it is recommended that this poem is used in conjunction with the DuelShock® controller.

PHIL BROWN

SIDE SCROLLER

WHEN 16 bits were enough for us
my friendship with my father was strongest.
When the sun was down and the dishes were done
we'd sit on my parents' double bed
playing *Streets of Rage*;
I would be Axel, he'd always be Blaze.
Humming to the MIDI melodies
we saw off hoards of hoods
jump-kicked punks and plucked
their fallen machetes from the floor
eating apples and turkeys from bins
vanquishing the denimmed unjust from factories
boats, brides and rationed our use of the A-Button
until a boss, and only then with quorum.
And when, me on my last legs, his Blaze died
midfight with Mr. X
I floundered without the aid of a Player 2
but he taught me the strength
to fight to my final Continue.

ALIYA WHITELEY

GROAN

> Look what we found
> in the park in the dark
> We will take him home
> We will call him Clark.
>
> *One Fish, Two Fish, Red Fish, Blue Fish,* Dr Seuss

CLARK, my friend, has a non-working leg.
He won't do a wheelchair.
He swells his arms with heavy weights:
up down, up down;
he drags himself around on sticks –
down to the pool, up to the park.
Clark rules. Clark is skill,
not least because he suffers.

We spend our cider-heavy nights
shooting the screen, zombie-beheading,
conquering death and his gammy leg.
Our trigger fingers grow slippery.
At the end of the secret laboratory and four cans of Strongbow
Clark needs a pee.
I watch him drag himself away
and hear the heave as he lifts himself
on to the porcelain throne.

Quietly
the night finds me in unfamiliar territory.

Delighted, it squeezes in bad thoughts
and packs them down tight.
In the fresh sudden silence of the flush comes a groan.
Stop mucking about, I say out loud.
I'm talking out loud to Clark, to the dark.

Just who is Clark? Is he a friend?
Or should I twitch my trigger finger?
When he comes round the corner, smile in place –
Look at you, look at you pissing your pants –
I try to laugh.
I shoot the zombies, through the night:
I make them extra-dead.
In the morning I go home to my room
and for the next month I make excuses.
Busy tonight. Double maths.

Years later I find
I'm not proud of my inability
to delineate the living
from the dead.

DAVID FLOYD

※

DALEY THOMPSON PLAYS DALEY THOMPSON'S SUPERTEST ON A ZX SPECTRUM EMULATOR

▟▙ The old flickery Daley is now much more solid and the backgrounds are more
pleasantly coloured.

REVIEW IN *SINCLAIR USER*, APRIL 1986

IN THOSE days of course
it took ages to get started.
You had to check the wires
were all plugged in right
shove in the tape
then try to time it so
you pressed play just
at the correct moment.
Half the time it screeched for a few minutes
then just stopped. I spent hours sitting there
waiting for it to load
When you did get it to load
it was all about pushing it to the limit
smashing the joystick left and right as
fast as you could without cracking the base
or snapping the suckers of the bottom
They don't have suckers on joysticks now, do they?
It's all this hand-held rubbish.
I remember one time
I'd lost my first two lives on the ski jump

but somehow I managed to get all the way through
to the spring board diving on my final life
I wasn't a great diver and I knew
it was make or break
so I really went for that dive
trying to complete three somersaults
before I hit the water
I pressed down so hard on the desk
that I pulled it over, brought it all down on top of me
and the monitor landed on my ankle
Kept me out for three weeks
almost missed the Olympic trials
It's not the same on this thing, is it?
Not the same. So fast.

SIMON BARRACLOUGH

SOLDIER OF FORTUNE

You WERE scandalised by the latest game,
the twenty-six separate zones of hurt
they'd mapped onto the human frame.

Pump head to stump,
leave limbs unhinged,
blow bowels outside,
make torso of a paragon.

What a piece of work is a man,
and precisely whose pieces are these?

"Remember, it's just pixels."
You counter: "It's disgusting." And then,
"Do you get to use a knife?"

RICHARD WATT
PIT BOSS

Pɪᴛ ʙᴏss, head of snakes
Shao Kahn eats bones
like nothing on Earth;

At three he stabbed a jewel
into his father's guts
for Outworld fame;

A black magic coven of hopes
look for a red singer
and announce him now;

Pearl-wood arms,
teeth like giant callipers
or perfect badger traps.

S.J. FOWLER
GOLDEN AXE

WE ALL of us sew for power

for choice

woman   man   dwarf

the bread of conserve

atives

I too want a guinea

equatorial, courage

trinity

the sweet warm flesh

of pressing south

to the grain

hot, & smelling

ruined

by what is next

the death adder

one had bitten himself

at the auction

a decade on

an heir to decay

merely one part of the underworld desolation

compelled to find refuge

wherever the destruction

had not yet been achieved

at least not in the invisible for

it is the sun

that the children of the tribe

contemplate

MULTI-PLAYER
VERSUS POEMS

PLAYERS

Kirsten Irving

Abigail Parry

RULES

In these poems, each player chooses a 'character' – this can be a real or fictional entity. The title then takes the format of 'Character 1 vs Character 2'.

The players take turns to write a couplet, writing three each in total. Aside from the opening stanza, the first line of each couplet must 'noun' all the verbs in the second line of the preceding couplet. So if the preceding couplet's second line includes the verbs 'wake' and 'reflect', for example, the first line of the next couplet should use 'wake' and 'reflection' as nouns. This action simulates 'blocking' or rejecting the actions of your opponent in a classic beat 'em up.

Player 2 does not need to continue the poem started by Player 1 – this is a poem of competing voices. Player 2's stanzas should be marked out from Player 1's by use of an indent and italics, and should form their own competing poem, interwoven with Player 1's.

SREDNI VASHTAR VS DOLORES 'LOLITA' HAZE

C'MON, let's hit the town. With my chiselled spit-and-fricatives
And your weird charm, we'll own the place by dawn.

> *It was strange, having an owner for so long, as if*
> *he'd rescued me from something, then buckled my collar.*

You didn't need a rescuer. The day the buckle chafes,
Slip the belt. Just wriggle and use your teeth.

> *We both loathed slips. No use for me, and his wriggler*
> *grew impatient when faced with layers, though pleats were fine.*

Grown-ups think it's clever, being tame. They learn faces
Off by heart, and trim their nails, and lose their bite.

> *I last saw him as grey as his waistcoat trim, limp, the loss*
> *of me in every crow's foot. And I didn't care. I didn't care a bit.*

DARIA MORGENDORFFER VS DEIPHOBE

YOU KNOW, we don't have to do this dance. I mean,
there's a Mutant Nephew Special on. Sit down.

> *I didn't ask for this: my existence a mere sit-in*
> *Through each ruthless, doldrum age. I bore myself.*

So school's one glorious bore, but at least there's someone
to snipe with. It's less fun to spread the scorn solo.

> *I have a sniper's range. From here, the years are just a spread*
> *Of fancy, flimsy cards. Pick one. I'll tell you what it says.*

We've got our pick, our say. We could be beautiful bank tellers
if we put our minds to it. We're not confined by ambition.

> *Free will? That's just a put-on, I'm afraid. Confinement*
> *To one fate is all you get. Now cut the deck.*

END OF LEVEL BOSS

WOMEN WHO FIGHT

CAMMY WHITE

Tʜᴇ ᴅᴇɴɪᴢᴇɴꜱ of Pellucci's do not see a victim of terrorist brainwashing. They see a girl with a menu, imperious as an impossibly stacked plate of pancakes, straight-backed as a competition sunflower. Who could guess that she was once programmed to kill at the tilting of her lover's brow? There is no clue in her long pigtails, which are curtain cords twitched by a child hiding. Nor in the cicatrice flickering on her cheek. The thong leotard she is most famous for is absent, or else worn beneath an outer façade of street clothing.

Cammy looks up at me from the menu:

"Perhaps you could not recite your introduction out loud," she suggests.

I acquiesce, and the interview begins. We discuss her exploits, her struggles, her regrets. She orders scrambled eggs on toast. All the time my Dictaphone whirs contentedly. I worm my way back toward the subject of the leotard, taking care to note that she is, in fact, not out of place in a fighting tournament consisting chiefly of men in smalls, shorts, mawashi or taleguilla, mostly bare-footed.

"There are also manifest practicalities," she adds. "Think of gymnasts, swimmers, dancers, divers…"

And the camo-paint straddling her much-remarked-on legs?

"Psychological impact" – and with the thumbing of her waistband, she shares with me and the woman opposite the tiny 'kill markings' she has begun to add, as on the noses of fighter planes, to her right thigh.

Now, of course, I'm noticing her eyes, and how each dark iris is like the pattern of data on a disk, wiped and written over again and again. Not blank but smudged to a vagueness. And how these round, wet palimpsests seem to be entreating something from me as we talk. Then it hits me – how much we need each other. How all she wants is someone to remind her she's a woman. The way she now looks away, toying with a pigtail in her lap – I take it for a brazen overture. I lean in for the kiss

[…]

and wake up in hospital, a pink bootprint still visible across my face.

TYRIS FLARE

Lacking the means to secure an appointment, I surprise Flare at her camp in the Schwarzwald after several days' tracking. But 'surprise' hardly seems the word. She emerges, mud-scorched and stinking, her flanks scrawled with minor lacerations, a hulking shrug of boar across her shoulders. The whole forest seems to yield her, like a breath it cannot hold. The root-strewn earth creaks like a beam, as if her every step threatened to collapse it.

Ignoring the press card I thrust at her, she sets the freshly murdered beast down beside the ash of last night's fire. I try to make the puzzle of scars across her body relate to a map I might have seen or could plausibly imagine. I know little of her history. She lost her parents to a marauding dark lord's armies, but where she comes from, such harsh experiences are the clay of everyday existence.

"I would not talk of it. Ask no more, bard of the mundane."

Now I'm sitting near her, I find that she's a burning bulb, kicking out more heat than the infant fire she is nurturing. To think, all that shields me from this heat is a smattering of cloth at those points where her nerve endings congress most busily. Her bra (what else to call it?) is a thing held together by a stained metal ring, and so sweated-in that each small cup seems as a crucible through which an acrid mineral is eating.

A different tack: I tell her that she has become a popular target for the underground *ryona* community. I explain *ryona* to her, putting it like so:

"...a sexual complex related to hurt or wounded women."

Videos of her being brutally set upon by orcs are shared on the internet. How does she feel about this? I hold my Dictaphone out pointedly, but she brushes it aside, grunting softly and continuing to work the fire.

Then it hits me – naturally, a woman like Flare thinks little of the subtle art of conversation. Instead, she expects to be conquered. No doubt she will boast of her feats and deeds at length, and more besides, once I have survived a night in her bed. Before me, a thousand crippled journalists have limped home, utterly defeated in the arena of physical love. Now the time of my own testing draws near.

With a dull knife, she begins to skin the boar, saying, "I suppose you expect me to share my meat with you?"

A brazen overture. Knowing what's expected of me, that I will have to take the first kiss by force, I approach her purposefully

[...]

and wake up in hospital, legs shoddily sewed back on.

The martial artist Mai Shiranui, who has duelled Vanessa many times in the King of Fighters tournament, is infamous for one reason only: the freedom her costume affords her breasts, recalled by some as 'like children's heads in a sack' or 'two stones in a trebuchet sling'. It seems apposite then to ask Vanessa, expert pugilist that she is, whether women fighters are ever of a wont to hoof each other in the chest.

"'Athena sped after Aphrodite with a will, and made at her, striking her on the bosom with her strong hand so that she fell fainting to the ground.' Book 21 of *The Iliad*," she says.

She has dropped her children at the crèche and rendez-voused with me in the clattery sort of café on the ground floor of the shopping centre. Her London bus bob is recently shorn, and sheer as a cathedral vault. For someone whose pelvic girdle has been tested by multiple instances of childbirth, her hips appear remarkably clenched. And although she pours whisky from a pewter flask into her coffee, she has the complexion of a freshly skinned apple.

I ask her if she feels she sets standards impossibly high for other women.

"You don't get to turn us against one another like that," she says, firmly.

And what of her brief appearances in non-fighting games – romantic love simulations in which the protagonist must 'date' one of a choice of women?

"I was only in one, as a side character. So you couldn't 'date' me. And it was in my contract."

As I look down my question sheet, she remarks that the only purpose of this interview seems to be 'to catch me out'. Then a waiter, in the midst of tossing some jovial remark over his shoulder, encounters the jutting edge of our table and sends coffee swirling across Vanessa's white shirt. Of course his eyes swell in horror and a dozen apologies try to force themselves out of his mouth all at once.

"It's all right," Vanessa says, applying a napkin and nodding in my direction. "This guy can buy me a replacement."

Then it hits me – why would a married woman agree to meet a hack like me in the middle of the day, only to cut across most of his questions? It only makes sense if she was looking for something else out of the deal. I'm not kidding myself – of course I'm just another bored lay to her. She can take it or leave it. Question is: should I take it?

Oh no, I think. I'm not falling for this a third time. But when she hauls me to the nearest clothing boutique and stands facing away from me, riffling through a rack of blouses, it's one brazen overture too many. I turn her round, readying my lips

[...]

and wake up in hospital, silver as a hologram with bruising.

ERI KASAMOTO

You see, it's the way we bring our children up. To a boy, every women is a mesh of living person and terrible, beautiful myth. He's heard of these things she stows about herself. Heck, he's seen them, but only in clandestine circumstances. These things are half outlawed, half promised to him. And here they are, actually occurring beneath the clothes of the person with whom you are speaking! A shifting rubble or secret collection, an intricate dollhouse of unique and windowless rooms. No wonder we are driven to sanctioned and unsanctioned mania.

I hope my little monologue strikes a chord with Kasamoto, but I doubt she hears me at all, so intent is she on firing our last signal flare in the direction of a smudge that might be a ship. The life raft lurches uncomfortably, as if the surface of the water were a swallowing larynx. Blackened by smoke and oil, Kasamoto's shoulders and collarbone nevertheless shine like polished obsidian. Her scraped knees coruscate with blood and her singed hair flickers in partial moonlight as she slugs what I take to be Polish *spirytus* from a canteen.

"Is it a case of a new shirt for every mission, or do you industriously bleach and sew them until there's more thread than shirt?"

She ties a knot in the torn strap so that the left side no longer sags. I listen attentively, since she has confiscated the batteries from my Dictaphone in case she needs spares for the torch.

"This one? This shirt is a goner. Other times they're salvageable."

"And how are you with sewing anyway? I mean, since you didn't have a mother and all."

Kasamoto shakes her head exhaustedly and looks back at the might-be-ship. As it transpires, it really is a ship – a Japanese squid jigger – and within ten minutes it has drawn up alongside us, bringing the little raft precariously close to capsizing. Once on deck, with our bodies thoroughly involved in towels, Kasamoto relinquishes the batteries to my care and allows the interview to continue.

"You're a trained special forces operative. Don't you worry that when you retire, you'll still want to kill people?"

"Some people. But I'm fairly good at not killing too."

Ironically, I have one of her hobbies listed as 'swimming'. Now, her shoulders dry and the oil, if not lifted, at least smeared to a thin varnish, she begins to take apart her pistol, the make of which I cannot identify with my still-bleary eyes.

Then it hits me – I mean, it really hits me this time. Douglas Syndrome: a temporary romantic bond between two people who have recently helped each other through an ordeal. Kasamoto must feel it too. As she shivers violently beneath her towel, I go to clutch her still-slick shoulders, pull her close to me

[…]

and wake up in hospital, still tasting seawater, a flake of bullet fluttering in my shin.

I-NO

I forego interviewing the formidable Baiken Seishino. Although I'd looked forward to meeting this one-armed, one-eyed, pipe-chewing swordswoman in the flesh, with my recent wounds flaring at the thought of any edged metal and my article still in a skeletal state, I decide it is safer to call in every one of my favours and exhaust every contact in search of I-No the axe witch, about whom little is known.

She is too much for any gaze – with platforms to shatter fire and the quality of seeming always to be a giantess stood seven hills away. If black magic were to ruthlessly detoxify its brand, it would create I-No. Broom swapped for semi-acoustic Gretsch, black tatters for top-to-toe rose-red leather, wart for a beauty spot. A part of you hopes for her to stumble and come apart, revealing herself to be all edifice, but stubbornly she's held together by that patina of semi-flushed skin.

"Does it chafe?" I ask. "All that leather?"

Whereupon her witch's hat, which has a stitched face and voice of its own, urges her to 'kill it'. But I-No, with the compassion of someone utterly untouchable, kneels to where I wrestle with my chains.

"It's comfortable," she says.

She has the guitar propped against her shoulder, ready to bring it down like a fairground hammer on my head. Again, her crooked hat insists, 'kill it', but I-No shushes it.

"You think you want to understand," she says, "but you don't. You think you're prepared to accept some of the blame, but you're not. You think you can get it out of your system, but you can't."

Then she sits on me, her leather creaking, the blunt club-head of her left femur just palpable through a cushion of haunch. Three feet away, my Dictaphone's little whirlpools go on turning, drawing in only husks of her words and the odd scrit – her fingernails stroking the guitar's strings. What I want to say I can only grunt:

"Would you do me a favour, I-No? Would you make a brazen overture, then imagine I tried to kiss you?"

[...]

I wake up in hospital, my face stitched into a permanent grin.

PLUCK &

STAGE TWO

PLUNDER ISLAND

MELISSA LEE-HOUGHTON
♡
HOT PURSUIT

I THIRST

LITTLE shivers of delight
sling the backpack into the lagoon
all the totem poles in the world
can't change fate,
or fight never-bruising skin
I'm too fat to swing in those trees
I will hold my breath
because you're so noisy
all the animals in the place come
rocking and swooping and pawing
there's no larking around with you
killing tigers, boars, bats
with your silver pistols
whipped from the black holsters on your
still juvenile thighs
shine a flashlight in my eyes
raise my temperature like influenza
when I can't make you go my way,
you climb beams
the sound of your thighs
and your knees against the wood is obscene
those pretty fingers get so torn
you don't thirst
I love that about you

no need for beauty therapists or analgesics

you make me nervous –

shooting at the walls

you want to go it alone

the lure of land, your booted soles

bouncing –

trouble comes like the straight arrow

of an absent heart

we talk it through

there must be a way

to open this door

of course there must,

why else would you be wearing hot-pants

in darkest Peru

and the hounds of hunger

pursuing

if I go with you

mystic, full-on, weakening

I come down with a fever,

my ordinary heart –

little shivers of delight

II LET DOWN

tender shoulders squared off snub
ache in the spine like cracked plaster
alabaster down the flanks
dare gun metal, slung low
and slung over the shoulder blades
smooth as marzipan and
terrain is fickle and bent
you turn it looks the same,
run into the walls in panic
Kali and Shiva hacked into the rock
dead as doornails
your time has come
deep in your virtual body heat
blisters have formed
lichen spoils all over your broken hands
you start to slip here,
slip there, and when
the tigers' teeth are in you
and you shake them loose you heal
so quick I can hardly mouth your name
blinking moon and stars come down
you can touch the sky
no bones just cartilage
moving rocks with your bare hands

I need paracetamol
freak show, wasp waist
tennis smash arms, pole dancer's legs
and if you don't get your medicine
ten more hours of this
I'll be knocked out, mute and you'll be
swinging from the vines like Tarzan
neutral
my hands react to your rage
like my body reacts to hot water
if we go back to the start
bludgeoning and bludgeoning
look out
when I leave you're dead
you're very dead

III Lara

you're never wet
the water is liquid nitrogen, seething
you don't breathe hard
yesterday I broke both of your legs and you snuffed it
not slippery, fallen, supple as ripe fruit
when they find you they will cut off your long plait
and feed your body to the wolf-cubs
only you were never there –
marauding
fluid as valium, and I don't break my heart
so you can go fucking around near waterfalls
stray bullets flying
that perfect brow and I'm
in my pyjamas and the elastic's gone,
you and I both know that door's not going to open
you gasp for air,
your skin never changes colour
I'm red round the eyes and my mouth is raw
as a sucked lollipop
your lips don't pucker
put me to shame with those pins
hacking at my legs with a blunt razor
where are your delicate veins

and your white lies and your adrenaline –
just inch toward me –
here, I will move you,
orphan

JON STONE

CALIGULA PREPARES TO JOIN THE PARTY

But lo, the party haven't turned up yet!
And all the food gone off. The billionth time,
him slouching in his throne, no TV set
to mitigate the castle's charmless gloom.
Just the checklist, which he checks: "Um, um,
yes." He ticks the ticks that mark more ticks.
Mystic items? Dozens. Weapons? Stacks.

He's got the golden armour, head to toe
– or rather, Burgonet to Sabaton –
and gold enough (it's been field-tested) to
smite the unsheathed eyes of anyone,
holy or unholy, with a shorn-
off glint of sun, unless they've goggles on.
And then there's this, which he has dubbed 'Ms Joan':

a polearm with a mecha-morphic head.
A swizzle of the quillons and a glaive
becomes, with much crunching of gears, a hide-
skinning svärdstav, or, if you've the nerve,
a straight blade for that close-but-long-range shave.
And since the thing's appropriately warlike
it doesn't matter that it's kind of phallic.

He's got the look, the pantheon of hair
(and hence won't often wear the Burgonet),
a bloody neckerchief, a cape, a scar.
He's got the motive: must avenge the lot.
Father, mother, sister for a start.
Then brother, other brother, step-dad, wife,
baby daughter – all the flags of grief.

He's picked out his romantic interest:
the little summoner with snowdrop flesh,
lightly armed and only lightly trussed
in – what, a star-embroidered shift, a sash? –
she could be jingled free from in a flash
of breath. He wants his long jaw prickled by
that shaved spot just before each beam of thigh.

Thanks to all that 'French art' from the East
he knows what follows is unduly gooey.
Never mind though. Once they're done and dressed
he'll cast a spell to clean them. Then he'll play her
theme song on his lute and she'll say, "Whoa."
But note: though he can strum a bristling chord,
his class is 'knight'. He's not some spoony bard.

They'll come, of course. They've got to. It is written
in the book or something. He's their man.
Deeply wronged/impassioned/wounded/smitten,
all the omens purring: "It's your turn!"
All the stones that weigh your carcass down.
The candles bite. The banquet table rots.
He waits. And waits. And waits. And waits. And waits.

E.KRISTIN ANDERSON
♡
THE INDEPENDENT CONTRACTOR

I AM A plumber – you wouldn't guess
from the jobs I perform these days.

And thankless, too! Money
is a headache, and my client
never where she says she'll be.

I need a change of clothes. I need
something to eat that won't get me
arrested back home. Meatballs, maybe.

My overalls are scorched.
I have a goddamned concussion.

Bills are piling up and it's just me
and my brother at home. Not enough
of us to form a union, get benefits.

And my client, she was supposed to be
the biggest benefit of all. I just need a good
plumber she said. Really, a handyman.

And I, being a 20th century do-it-yourselfer
and gentleman, well, I believed her.

♡
THAT METROID GUY IS A LADY

I NEVER played the game myself –
no balls, you might say. But I watched
one afternoon, a cohort's 8-bit victory;
we should have been outside.

He hummed the theme as he played,
a man, muscles in a musty dorm room.
But panel after panel, it was peace.

He knew the surprise ending, hinted
as the old controller squeaked in his hands.
Had I known this warrior's legacy, I'd have seen it too,
might have lamented the downslide of, say, wardrobe.

It seems the third dimension has made way
for the salacious. And Samus was not consulted
anymore than I was. Then, beckoned to watch:

This last scene, game won,
helmet off, one step for chicks.

CHARLOTTE GEATER
♡
DRAGON THEORIES

& THE ANGLO-SAXONS frazzled   soaks in the dark.
coughs in the green wood   but no phlegm croaks,
curled supine /   curled i saw dying rotten

& in the sky, dragons.   cold fists & hearts
they sparred damp chests   all the kings
were young men & all   the kings fell down.

& so we draw what they strained   for
new slants for language not   thunder
& scales, bones, scrawled legs   kicking

so there are we making it real hi god
it's me charlotte mud for nails & we're busy
writing old books pushing the spaces
out retyping & creaking the names on the
spines wulfswith aethelstan w/scales for yr
eyes & our hands pass through yours
wishing we could feel the heat there.

BEN WILKINSON

♡

LINK'S AWAKENING

Long weeks lost at sea in your little boat
caught in the gathering storm of yourself
you cling to the mast and dwindling hopes
as lightning transforms all to darkness.
You wake: the surf's spray across your face,
weird bird calls, the faint smell of coconut,
a soft, familiar voice … What is this place?
Stranger than you could ever believe it,
though the islanders call it Koholint –
these beaches, lakes and forests that ring
a dark, uncharted mountain. You set out
in the vague hope of unravelling things,
but find the waves never far from your ear.
Is that owl watching you? Why are you here?

NIALL CAMPBELL

THE PLAYER LOST IN GANON'S TOWER

Returning to a room I find
exactly what I'd found before:
the same small beast, alive again,
the same green gem of its loss;

the architectural preference
for stonewall and stone walkway;
and then, as always, this dead-end
of my stuttered quest.

I take out my blue flute and play
that one and only song it knows
for the key I'm still to find, the door
I haven't found to open –

These are times when my doubts recur
as cloud-cover on a day for clouds –
that all my maps lead to nowhere;
that the town is burnt and ruined;

that when my back is turned, Link
might hunker down in the silence,
as Theseus did before him, and listen
to the pointlessness of it all.

CHRISSY WILLIAMS
♡
LISTENING TO MIDNA

P<small>LACES LIKE</small> this are always full of holes.
You aren't a human now. You're a beast.
I'll make you a deal. Look up at the sky!
I doubt you're used to your body. I'll show you.
That won't work. Give up. Don't you hear me?

      Places like this are always full of holes.
You were never human. You're just a beast.
What deal do you want? To keep the sky?
Let me show you your body. I can use it.

      Places like this are always full of holes.
You're barely human at all. You're a beast.
There are no deals left. The sky is destroyed.
Let me doubt your body. I'll make you do it.
Nothing now will work. It won't. Give up.

      Places like this are always full of holes.
Humans run away from your beastlike self.
The deal is the sun can no longer see the sky.
I doubt you'll ever know how to use your body.
Nothing will ever work. Give up. Give out.

      Places like this are always full of holes.
You won't miss the memory of humanity.
You'll soon find you don't miss the stars.
No one will ever ask to see your body.

      Places like this are always full of holes.
Dark beasts continue to welcome you.
The dark sky. Your darkness. The stars, dark.

Places like this are always full of holes.
Evil humans are beasts. There are no humans.
The dark sky deals only in our death.
Never show people a body they can't use.
Places like this are always full of holes.
Your beast's mind will remember nothing.

♡ ROBOT UNICORN ATTACK

Possibility bursts like a horse
full of light, accelerating
into a star. Explosion. Hit
<X> to make your dreams
crash into stone. Death.
Diatonic chimes of joy.
I want to be with you.
Let dolphins fly in time.
Swim through air, leap
past sense, past sin and then
hit <Z> to chase your dreams
again. Always. Harmony. Up,
smash goes the rainbow-trailing
heart again. Again. Again, again!
I want to be with you when
make-believe is possible.
I want to be with you when
robot unicorns never cry, hit
stars collapse in quiet love.
When there is only love.
Harmony. No shame.

♡

MIRROR, OKAMI, STARDUST

I HAVE never enjoyed running so much
　　as when I have my white wolf's paws under me
　　　　drumming the earth, showering blossom.

I have never enjoyed swimming so much
　　as when I kick stardust in my wake,
　　　　creating waves of stars to light the sky.

I have never enjoyed nature so much
　　as when pollen flies to mark the delight
　　　　of cats and canine warriors I have fed.

I have never enjoyed dying so much
　　as when a mirror of stone, bone and wood
　　　　returns me to my purest state, offers a second chance.

JOE DUNTHORNE
♡
DEAR JAFFAR,

LIQUEFY me now or these impossible hips
will arrange themselves on your princess.
I will pour through your dungeons, half-Slinky,
half-thief. You can't seriously think
that she'd fall for you, a sultan with only two
styles of attack. I'll be there in the hour,
no stains on my *lungi*. Our showdown,
that letdown, will end with your body
reduced to a heap. Not even this damnable
sprite collision can stop us from placing flesh
upon flesh. We will be made new,
conjoined by a limited palette. The same colour
that blushes my cheeks will also burn on hers.

PHIL BROWN
♡
SONIC SENRYU

A BLUR of lapis
lazuli bursts to collect
one more emerald.

Helicopter fox
spins a white diameter
always just off screen.

A pink echidna
knuckles swollen from the climb
loses his last ring.

Dr. Robotnik
opens a letter: 'Never
work with animals...'

S.J. FOWLER

ALTERED BEAST

A COOKED goose, born blind
resurrected by zeus
into a sofa, spirit & flesh of the lean
the lamb
dis
of she loves
as ours is all flowers
centurion as a runner
& those officers shall not delay me from me
Uday! I still remember you
integral part of our recent history
sons & daughters
splatters of the atom
diseased whore, a bus full of free seat
& where do you sit? & how much
did they steal?
did they cough the air black?
too a lust for power
hermaphroditic hatred
Neff of the captured Athena
silver silk ties to power bases in the middle Rome
a dancing, twisting, turntable matador
the silver beast
a hairs blood & horror just everywhere

♡
DONKEY KONG

TO CHARTER a plane, to hire a pilot
the prefiguring of project Nim, a sign language of love
a father raising his sons in battle, to barrels
a raising above ones head the bad waves of black water

where will forgiveness hide when I need you?
inside the closed fist, the meat of hammer
landing heavy, letting loose, flirting with rollers
scaling ladders with princesses, to save them from themselves

they, not we, are the forgiving, the knowing
within the myst of a rally, of a crusherrrr
animals who have suffered experiments, vaccines
they will forgive us in the wake of his vengeance

RICHARD WATT
♡
DRAGON'S LAIR

Death is Hell
and gaping wide;
Dirk removes his mail
to scrape a wiry wrist
between the floorboards of an empty house –
ever searching for a deeper thing.

Down,
down the coastal path
to caves and fifty killers;
along the gunflint trail
old man sea lines his pockets
while the crumbling coast's
a song of silence
dreamed of by eroding stones.

Into the forest with hackles and axes:
spurs chink on lichened flagstones where
weeds die under foot: he's brown as blood
running low and accurate, over skulls.

Glinting in the verge betrays
his previous helms.

Vines have no taste
but boughs bend to him

and give up their lowest fruit.
Stop – silence – traps –
geese startle in the bracken
as a speaker in the leaves,
conduit for Singe,
spits the no-quarter verdict
mid-leap, mid-swing:

"You're just a shit kid
from a single swing park town
lost between arcades.
You'll never make that gap
but I bid you, try again."

ROSS SUTHERLAND
♡
GAUNTLET

⁕ The original *Gauntlet* was released with no ending. The hundred or so levels were randomised and looped for as long as play lasted. Atari saw *Gauntlet* as a process, a game that was played for its own sake and not to reach completion. The adventurers continue forever until their life drains out, their quest ultimately hopeless.

GAMASUTRA.COM

I. ELF

ELF, MY heartiest congratulations on reaching level 130! What unbelievable progress you've made. What a glittering career. I bet you look back on the previous 129 indistinguishable levels and find it hard to believe how far you've come. Have you considered writing a book about your travels? All those rousing tales you must have about walking through a series of identical rooms. I know a publishing house that may well be interested. Why, I imagine it will be the sleeper hit of next summer. As soon as your prodigious adventure is over, why don't I set up a meeting? I'll invite a couple of television executives as well, and perhaps Sam Mendes, and the Archbishop of Canterbury. You'll forgive us if we all chant "Elf! Elf! Elf!" when you enter the restaurant. We're all dying to meet you, Elf! In fact, I believe the people of Britain are planning some sort of standing ovation for you when you finally reach the edge of the dungeon. Assuming, of course, that there is an edge to the dungeon, which there isn't.

2. WARRIOR

Don't listen to me, Warrior. Please, continue to let your naive sense of purpose pilot you like a crummy, pixelated ghost ship through a grey sea of nothingness. I have no doubt that you will 'hold the course', Warrior, much like a man falling off a roof, or a blaring car-horn trapped under a corpse. No one can doubt that your trajectory is immaculate, Warrior, unblemished by reality. I have just put the finishing touches on a mural that illustrates your many adventures. Here you are, picking up dog mess off a busy street, wearing a paper bag on your head with a crudely-drawn crown upon it. I call it "The System That You Cannot See And Yet So Cowardly Protect". Perhaps you would like to destroy it and prove my point.

3. WIZARD

Wizard, as an ironist, you alone receive some sense of subjective freedom. Your outré dress sense deprives your surroundings of a finite degree of cognitive reality. In this manner, the dungeon can never truly hold you. Perhaps you expect us to be grateful for this mockery. Perhaps you would like us to bake some sort of special cake in your honour. How privileged you are, Wizard, and yet your surreal brand of comedy is just as reductive as the boilerplate ethics it attempts to negate. Deep down you have never truly questioned the rules. I will wager that you have never had an original thought in your life. How ironic, Wizard, that you are incapable of fantasy. Your only escape will be from your own bloodstream, and even then your raft will never reach the rim of the ocean.

4. VALKYRIE

They say that the show is never over until the fat lady sings (and you, Valkyrie, are unmistakably that fat lady). However, this particular rendition of Götterdämmerung is undergoing a series of dramatic rewrites at the behest of your controversial composer, a clownish horror of a man, who is composing a series of new librettos by headbutting a photocopier. An acknowledged unusual choice of collaborator (and one who many feel has outstayed its welcome at the Vienna Volksoper), the photocopier continues to be associated with the opera house due primarily to its prolific output, with you and your fellow singers receiving new pages every day, and although the sheets are all identical, featuring instructions on how to milk dogs, you and your ensemble remain grateful for the work, spending every minute of your waking day trying to bring the text to life, pushing Wagnerian harmony further and further with extreme chromaticism and generous use of dissonance, the production stretching out over days, weeks, years, until eventually the baritone is shot dead by the Slovene conductor Hugo Franck, and the renowned tenor Marco Casolini dies of malnutrition. Indeed, it looks unlikely that you will be winning the Nilsson Prize any time soon. One might even start to form the opinion that the entire production is a sham and a valuable mezze-soprano's talents would be better-suited elsewhere, for example, face-down at the bottom of a swimming pool. Sure enough, spend long enough at the grindstone and all the walls will start to look like exits. And nobody, Valkyrie – chubby monkey that you are – nobody can walk through that door like you can.

SAM BUCHAN-WATTS

THE OCTOBER REVOLUTION AND A GOLDEN CHOCOBO

THROUGH study guides latticed with Squaresoft manuals for the PS1,
you will – by chance – hack into a strategy risky by departure from known routine.
Pissed with stress, you will learn to love the calm in mealtime,
know your tendency for distraction like the menu-screen's pigment-blue.
Revision, and its subsequent reappraisal for everything
discounted for lack of immediate fun, becomes
searching the benign bits of Gaia for the best breed of Chocobo bird
you can only happen on by accident; let the minigame be meat in the RPG.

As perpendicular as the 4-disc case, sits your AS Level history
in a Xeroxed pamphlet, the red pack of facts.
Between these you will flit in hourly bursts of intrigue, from memory tactics
punching dates into the brain; the Treaty of Brest-Litovsk,
the abdication of the Tsar, Trotsky's master-
gameplans, will become interchangeable with Mideel, a
Zeio nut, the impact a Spencer and two Kyuvilduns
have on the mateability of an Ocean Chocobo.

At dusk, the bird you aim for will silhouette itself, shape an 'A' on the skyline,
getting starker with each day. Come dawn, his 'wark!' will rhyme with
your alarm.

And what now do you remember?

A history glitch you were told exclusively not to take to the exam room
you can recall far better for this fact: the revolutionary rule put
shortly on hold while a cretin lost the cabinet keys. That more veterans died,
hearty with the past, in Eisenstein's remake of the Red Palace storm
than they did in the heat of 1917. You could have cheated Choco-nature,
earned a gold one beating Ruby Weapon, had yourself a sprinter
at the Choco-Races, clamping up + down at once on the control-pad.
The incessant korgy funk of the Chocobo theme tune.

But look back to the bird through your skylight. Sentinel on the night.
See it defined, as striking in profile as Lenin was
against that wood podium – cap in hand, leant into the air: a frontier,
what looks to be a crashing wave. Find gold feathers in the surf.

CLAIRE TREVIEN

PAST SIMPLE

FLASH BACK to that time we walked down Greek Street,
your thumb crushing the vein at my wrist to
direct me into the heart of the reek.

I was lost: pressed against the dense tattoo
of a city. From printed cobbles, fonts
screamed: "Remember your shadow", a clue

to capture as you glided me beyond
the howling windows to the lisping taps
of a pub you said you'd be keen to haunt.

**

Inside the map, I can marvel at the fact
that I've lost your arm.
The sun burns sharper when I storm
right, then back.

I can rewind to the tube stop, where it began,
make us detach,
say that – I can't stay, hope you understand.
There's a show I have to catch.

CHELSEA CARGILL
♡
MANIC MINER,
48 KILOBYTES

In the abandoned
uranium workings
the main risk
is falling out of fright.

and *In the Hall*
of the Mountain King
will still be playing
in cut-out beeps

I don't know if
Chernobyl happened yet
or we were still
carving our names
into pencils
but you will always fall
in slow motion

You barely notice
the stop-motion wings
and seals spinning
beach balls on their noses.
A cavern alien
runs on clockwork.
Ground gives way

even with infinite lives
you jump into the next screen
and land on a monster
fall into a chasm
end in a flash
over and
over

SABRE WULF, CIRCA 1984

\SOMETIMES you manage to
reach the very edge
and there are mountains

\the screen turns black
into unending unstarry night

\sabre wulf dark age mass
parading hunted tusk omen
patrols back and forward
unseen in the depths

and a sleeping boar wakes

\you are only killed by
running for your life

♡
VALHALLA

\THE DEAD reappear with no word
of explanation

fights break out
between gods and giants

wolves, dwarves and ravens

\you die of hunger
then wake up in an icy wasteland

with the same forests,
marshes, lakes and plains

the same pixellated soup-dragon
that opens and shuts its jaws

in time to the march of its stick-feet

\the inside of a great hall
is just called *Hell*

you can order the gods around

\the point is to see
how many times
you can starve or pick fights
with giants

and be reborn

GABRIELLE NOLAN

I CO

THEY LOVED you, until
two white horns grew
from your head. The cherished son,
now ill-omened. Warriors
brought you to the empty castle,
put you in a stone box,
a sacrifice to the dark heart
of this island fortress.

But a quake shakes the earth –
cracks your coffin wide.
Springing loose, you run through
bare rooms. You find a girl
who shines bright as the moon.
From a suspended cage
you free her and take her pale
hand. She speaks softly
in a language you cannot
understand. You know
the castle can only be escaped
with the strength of two.

But she is slow, unsteady,
cannot leap or fight when
her mother's black beasts
embrace with vaporous limbs

and drag her down into the flagstones,
as if through quicksand.
You take her pale hand,
pull her up from the dark mass.
You climb, she follows.

HARRIET MOORE

DREAMS OF A HOUSE

I

THE NIGHT

SOME TIME after the pitch dark

an old man is undressing
forgetting the word for wife

reaching into his dreams to remember himself.

II

THE BUILDING

In his dreams

the past is something to be stepped out of,
a heap of clothes at the foot of the bed.

He imagines her folding years
and putting them away, freezing and defrosting
the days in Tupperware, getting them out for his
sons and daughters over Sunday dinner.

He saw this coming like the rain:

The building bending its knees to the ground,
and being emptied out, the building on its knees and empty.

III
THE DAY

This is where he is storing their dreams

He'd like to put them in the washing-machine, and hang them up to dry
to let their neighbours lift their blinds and see him returning

tired from a long journey, shifting the weight of the dark
on his back to be carried through the dawn for his wife.
In a stranger's clothes he is a different man,
he can fold the future in the palm of her hand like an inventory,
he can open the door of her dreams and speak:

I have gathered the night in the crook of my arm,
I can give you something complete

  like a house scooped out

        or a bed, a bathtub, a chair.

KIRSTEN IRVING

ARCADIA

⁋ Today Arcadia was closed off to all but paying customers. The man hires me to build a
forest at the bottom of the ocean, and then turns a walk in the woods into a luxury.

JULIE LANGFORD, *BIOSHOCK*

L OOK CLOSELY: you'll see the water above
projected in hula arms of light
across the leaves of this blue fan palm,
slipping down from our wet, shifting sky
to tickle an orchid's dragon tongues.

You get the feeling
something wants us to remember
the surface world? Here, miles beneath
the North Atlantic's waves, I can make you
the fattest, glossiest leaves.

I can make you a tree farm.
After all, we govern the weather.
We have tricked nature
into shunning the sun
and throwing its tendrils at electricity.

Oh, and aren't we so civilised?
Here in the tea garden, plucking crisp fennel,
screened from the commerce laying eggs

in the systems outside. Let us inhale,
drink, and forget for a moment.

The background hum
of the generators has become
the bees for us; the register of coin in slot
the rubbing of crickets' legs, but there is
nothing false about this leaf. Touch it.

When they close the hothouse doors,
having wafted a sniff of earth at you,
and ransom the grass, set against
the tombish iron corridors, we both know
we will pay whatever they ask.

KATE POTTS

DOOMDARK'S REVENGE

Doomdark leaks into the house
through a rotted angle of window frame.

The dusky scrape and hubble of him's
furred with a dandruff of gloss-white paint.

He draws in the ribs and sails of himself,
plants his manta ray body beneath

the settee and his one good eye rings out:
a peppered, indelible moon.

His claws rasp on the carpet's weave;
he squats, cold as cordite. While I am gone

he upsets the salt pot so that a sting
of crystals will slough my heels.

He gags sandy bile from his gut-depths,
coughs it in rivulets over the lino,

gnaws the furniture's edges and legs
to a snotty mash and draggle of fibres, peels

a shingle of wood pulp from the timber
of the kitchen door. Everything heaves, leans.

Dumb totem, he guards the back door,
still and implacable when I return.

I sit, sink. Doomdark clatters,
barks his low siren, cranks out blue sound:

a hounded, metallic whale. He springs, swipes
at the auricle of my ear with a scissor

of claw, then snaps back, jumpy as a ratter.
Now time's a stutter, a halt.

My fingers pinch at the bloody cartilage.
Oh the incessant intent of that one good eye!

He sees, for all the house's bleach and clean,
my wrongs, tied up in brittle muslin

under my liver – a pocket of growths, of moulds –
the dank cheese of them resting inside me.

MULTI-PLAYER
♡
PARTY GATHERING POEMS

PLAYERS

Matt Haigh

John Clegg

RULES

Instead of being against one another, here the players work collaboratively. As before, write in couplet stanzas. Each stanza should introduce a new 'hero' to the party, in the form of a character or creature (real, historical, mythical or fictional), taking their cue from some element of the second line of the previous stanza. The poem can simultaneously work as a narrative or other progression.

If two players are participating, they take it in turns and write two stanzas each. If four players are participating, they write one stanza each.

The last thing to decide is the title, which should be a collective name for your party responsive to the various heroes you have gathered.

TAROT

THE LOVERS fused, their shared hub of head a zygote
now of crystal bees, the same glistered grapefruit –

Your next draw discloses the soon-to-be-hanged man,
his drawn-out last breakfast, the noose of spooled honey –

Ruin, the meta-minotaur, glutted
on the thought balloons he's condemned to gore –

and lastly the Emperor's body double, a sackful of air.
You can shuffle again, if you like, but the clock is ticking.

ESPERS

I WAS the first cloud. I gulped a meteor
down. Blooding the sky, my self's lazuli butter.

My brother below me curls up at low tide
and by night time is nowhere. I reach through

his oil-dark face to spear awake our fallen
submerged sister, the heaven-smelling husk,

whose sleep throws up Indian ropes of steam
for her lost lover, all mist and misdirection.

POCKET DEATHS

Draw out the pins and blink awake.
I want a word with those dead friends of yours.

That Grandpa Munster breathing doll –
flush him from your pocket. Next, his cohorts,

taxidermied labrats clean and smooth
as snooker balls, Sundance and Stagger.

The boy who slew the mountain, cribbed his Gameboy
from its guts, requests a squad for his next job.

END OF LEVEL BOSS
♡
CENTO FOR
A NAMELESS ONE

❦ Planescape: Torment is so encyclopaedic that the parameters of the game, its aims
and its player's goals, remain dispersed or vague [. . .] Its limits are elusive.
    DIANNE CARR, 'GENRE AND AFFECT IN SILENT HILL AND PLANESCAPE: TORMENT'

❦ . . . Sigil, the City of Doors, where unpredictable portals link to multiple worlds.

❦ – Morte, why didn't you say something when we were at the mortuary?
    – Because I never know who you're going to be! Some of your incarnations have been
    stark, raving mad!

IN THE BEGINNING is your end.
It was dark and then it isn't.

The mortuary.
Inhaling and inhaling. Think of that pain,
to breathe in light and more and inhale again.

You are wearing neither helmet nor mail coat,
nor any breastplate or armour at all.
Mummies storm your torn insides
with their bandages and embalming honey.
You are autographed with darkening syllables.

Hey, Chief, you okay?

Propped in the shadow,
stalled on the still plain,
tongue quicker than
a beam – a head, naked of skin,
busy with invocations: clank of tankard, rattle of coins,
beautiful clacks in the wind:

Skanking rudegirl pull it off cool.
    Strange typhoons invade
        my boss.

You feel it most at night, how the earth turns cold beneath you,
agony under agony, the quiet of dust,
a sluggish tide, a small surprising wind.
The glorious dead, walking
barefoot on the earth.

You are not Prince Hamlet, nor were meant to be.

1) Do not arrange your bright flesh in the sun.
2) "What happens now, Mr Bones?"
3) "Put wine into my hand, my heart is tormented."

Black
like the memory-wound.
You wake up electrified out of the coma by your own soul's
borrowed falsetto.
Hallucinations of remembrance
and reconfronted detail: how
it's clear you're endlessly arriving – endlessly
wicked, rather than virtuous out of conformity or fear.
Is there an ur-dream, better than words, an almost
violent kind of delightfulness?

The atmosphere is not a perfume – it has no taste of the distillation.
It is odourless.

So   the firestorm   *(Ignus hears you)*
gathering the heat to himself, in one thermic
hazard. Torchlit smoulderer,
nose filled with steam & his brief cries,
both sun and firefly behind his shock waltz.

Forgive me my combing, forgive me my crawling, forgive me my fire.
No one is exempt
and everyone's pain has a different smell.

1) Go to the bank by the wood, and become undisguised and naked.
2) "Come, death. Do not be so slow."
3) "But who is stronger than death?"

Waking, needle-sharp and aching,
but several seconds later, truly waking,
the moon dangling wet like a half-plucked eye,
black the blood in its loud tunnel.
Carrion stars, charnel planets, carcass elements
corpse the universe.
Your shank-hooked heavy ham-shape is crustifying like a barnacled whale.
What was it for the longest time but lore, lure?
The mosquitoes are biting tonight
like memories.
The past recedes like an exaggeratedly long shadow.

Autumn wind
blasting the stone
of Ragpicker's Square.

Sigil: a weathered
skeleton,
spools of dark thread sewing the shadows together.

I hear your words.

Interior war. Uncomic harrow.
Carved in the heart
a rusting ring.
What unguents beat
through his polished tomb?

What alchemy forges
the ornamental waterfall?

1) Listen to the night's wind.
2) "And where have they gone? Where are they now?"
3) "I wish I could remember what its name was."

Waking at four to soundless dark, you stare.
Chartreuse blanquette, shirt lavender, frayed
    mustard thongs.
No cloud, no relique of the sunken day.

Looks like the dusties lost one of their deaders.

She's a lean vixen: you can see
the ribs, the sly
trickster's eyes, filled with longing
and desperation, the skinny
feet, adept at lies,
slick with humiliation when dismissed, hair
      wrapped in knots, secret purple liquid
in her circus fingers,
tail signing indelible annihilation.

Beauty breaks ground in strange places,
in the way that the most of the wind
happens where there are trees.

She is brittle as brimstone.
If you were a grub, you'd eat a hole in her.
Fog shroud
and clouds,
a moon of smoke.

This air,
she says, *feels as if it hasn't touched land*
for a thousand miles.

You are a ruthless man, devoid of all mercy.

Surely that is not your penis you hold in your hand?

1) "Which were the baths where they taught you to swim?"
2) Be the right man in the right place for once.
3) "Not on a night like this, sweet."

Slow awakenings	Flat arousings	Premature wakefulness
Extinguished reverie	Sifted dream	Perforated sleep

Deep
in the timecrevasse,
in the closed dinosaur shop,
in the honeycomb-ice,
waits a breathcrystal.
After many years of wandering,
your unalterable
testimony.

STAGE
THREE

BRAINTHUNDER
MOUNTAIN

CHARLOTTE RUNCIE
IN MY POCKET

" My heart is in my
pocket, it is Poems by Pierre Reverdy.

FRANK O'HARA

" Pikachu, I choose you!

POKÉMON

ELECTRIC fighting bug,
water, grass, and fire.
Six balled-up monsters
slung around my hips.

For now they must be fruit:
I palm one, feel the pores
and bowl, and blinking down
just when it splits

I splinter into anime.
A heart is shared in six:
a team of hearts in red-and-white
in jeans, my hand and pack,

caught systems of defence
once wild. Imagination loves,
jack-in-the-boxes fighting
from a pen made out of oranges.

ISOBEL DIXON
PINBALL ELECTRA

YOU AND YOUR robot bride, I scoff
(the sport of waking her, waking her),
cold metal clattering to fleshen
out the supine girl, evince
that throaty laugh's ideal
appreciation of your skill.

You ribbed me back –
how I, Electra-like, keep
harping on my theme.
And I dream a dark arcade,
where the pinball king
has made a game of genius,

to make him breathe, if
I play it right. Shake the cabinet
with the volleys, flippers
to defibrillate the dormant heart,
a silver hail on whitened skull.
Make him turn and see.

No cheat codes for this level,
a hall of earnest girls play on.
Coinfall after coinfall,
the expectation of that crucial voice,
shattering the case's glass.
Make him speak to me.

KIRSTEN IRVING
✿
PINBALL DREAMS

NIGHTMARE

SOMETHING STIRS me – a bat? – and I spring up, clocking my head on something hard and old. It's a tombstone. The smile left from last night, with you all tousled and obsessed, gunning for victory over the white hills of my body, dissolves in the clammy grass and the realisation that I am lying on top of a dead man named Harry Host. I lever myself up using his headstone, skinning my elbow, and look for you. The graveyard is lit only by fairy lanterns, put there by some thoughtful verger for the wicked and abandoned. I call your name and the sound is flung about like a drunk. I remember you promising to marry me, and I don't remember this place. I thought we were in Italy. As I turn, a cackle sneaks past and I pull my damp clothes tighter. Answer me, did you hide him? Did you take him home with you? The cold has glued itself to my bones, and I think I will just sit here a minute, feeling Harry at my back, saying that's right, you rest

BEAT BOX

I tumble towards the only open door. A sign above attempts to say *Viva*. I ask the doorman if he has seen my fiancé, and he repeats the charge for entry to his miserable palace, slapping me backwards when I try to bypass him. My money in his craw, he pulls aside a rat-gnawed purple rope to let me in. A disc jockey like a wizard is trying and failing to cast a charm from a pulpit near the ceiling. Bodies jig on the illuminated dance floor: with each beat and each step off, a square exhales and dies; when a heel hits home like a thump to the chest, the square gasps back into life. Elbows to the ribs, to the back, and nobody breaks rhythm. A glass hits me across the throat. Funny how much blood

Steel Wheel

I leap aboard as the whistle blows; someone said they saw you in the first class carriages, and you had grown a moustache. As the wheezy waltz of the train builds, I see your nape – nobody else has that twitch of hair in the shape of a question mark – vanishing into the dining car, and I race along the mahogany carriages, tossing children and men aside, ramming into the wall with each jolt. You are clearly in love and looking for me. I cry out that I am here and that you needn't shave; a moustache sits well with a groom's suit. The train lurches, throwing us forward, and the lamps flicker. My hat is dented, my skull a broken bowl. What's that? I need a drink – perhaps you will buy me

Ignition

As the countdown begins, I rush across the tarmac. You are a smudge on the window of the rocket. I cannot be sure it is you at all, but I cry out that I love you, that there is nothing to forgive, and that you needn't do this. They can send dogs. I trip over a wire and drop my ring, but get up to show you I can be strong for both of us. The suit they have given me is grey, like my hair, and I have used the grey anti-combustive face paint your colleagues recommended, so I understand if you cannot see me so clearly. The burners are fired and you are rising, but it's not too late. The flames are immense, look! I'm not even touching them and my skin is pinking. Perhaps I should dye my hair to match for the wedding. Darling, the invitations

TEN GREEN BOTTLES

She tells me she was a builder before all this. Before that, a miner. I have been staring at her flexed palm for an hour. In the distance, Francis has climbed a glowing cliff and walks towards the edge.

He's going to fall. Let me through, I beg. She shakes her mossy hair and holds her T-shape. Frank plummets, with a small cry, into chalk.

Mike begins to scale the side. I ask her again to step by. She nods towards the new mountaineer, who walks off the edge, but opens a yellow parasol and drifts down. *The gods are learning*, she says. And then Mike stops, over the other side, inches from escape, and spreads his arms like her.

Now, she says, and I find myself scrambling up the bright block. Which, I see now, has arrows pointing to her and the trapped hundreds.

We must start from the other side, she calls, *to get there at all. Now open your parasol.*

And I do. And as I float to the floor, the golden door is there, just beyond my steadfast predecessor.

You spoke to Marianne, Mike grunts, his fleshy blockade so like hers. *Do you want to save the others?*

He is such a different creature to the one who went up.

Yes, I want to save them.

Then turn around and dig.

As I start to claw, I hear muffled crying and scurrying: the others panicking that we will always be stuck here, chanting the names
of the dead and the missing.

I am not a miner like you, Marianne – help me, I shout into the stone face.
I am not a miner comes back.

Just as my stripped hands threaten to show bone, and my small heart nearly clocks out, an eye appears in the tunnel, and joy and feet flood it.

I can see it I can see the door is it true it's not a myth I see it too

They run as their robes will allow, towards freedom, towards Mike, who screams *STOP* and explodes.

And it's over the crumbs of his body they go:
It's the door it's the door at last woo hoo

I –

Marianne: *Go. GO, YOU IDIOT.*

So I do, and only when my hand is on the door frame, and I can smell grass, do I turn to see the countdown start above her head.

CLIFF HAMMETT

SNAKE

WATER sneaks between

the paving cracks

this pixel-thick snake

can neither find apples

nor eat its own tail

but will blossom a spray when

it reaches the road and

wheels

car

spinning

off

rebounds

CHRISSY WILLIAMS
❧
SONNET FOR ZOOKEEPER

CAPTURE the set number of animals to complete the level[1]

crocodile	drop	lion	delete	crocodile
drop	lion	delete	crocodile	drop
lion	delete	crocodile	drop	lion
delete	crocodile	drop	lion	delete
monkey	elephant	delete	swipe	monkey
elephant	delete	swipe	monkey	elephant
delete	swipe	monkey	elephant	delete
swipe	monkey	elephant	delete	swipe
chain	delete	panda	hippo	chain
delete	panda	hippo	chain	delete
panda	hippo	chain	delete	panda
hippo	chain	delete	panda	hippo
giraffe	swipe	drop	chain	giraffe
swipe	drop	chain	GAME	OVER

---

1. If you get tired, try pressing START to pause the game for a few seconds. Try looking away from the screen. Try staring at the ceiling and the shadows cast by the screen light. Try imagining you are driving at night on a stretch of road lit by ever-watching cats' eyes and have turned off your headlights.

HOLLY HOPKINS
✦
SAMOROST

¶ 'Samorost' in Czech means a root or piece of wood that resembles a creature; but it is also a term for a person who doesn't care about the rest of the world.

JAKUB DVORSKÝ, LEAD DESIGNER OF SAMOROST

THESE GOATS sing.
The overbite that rakes the grass
curls back and one by one they sound
as if they've swallowed glockenspiels;
notes float down the valley with the hawks.

There's a pit
where their jumbled bodies rot
when startled from their morning nap
bagpipe bodies clatter and fall.
The farmer has gone fishing off the cliff,
a gang of greying lizards climb the rocks.

...

There are many people in the wood
where yawning tree-boles make a face,
a curl of fungus sniffs the air,
the bark's dark fishers listen in.

Puffballs swim past in their white rubber caps.

...

You can tell it's real because there're flies
jutting back and forth, measuring the air,
checking the world has not been filled with glue.

A snail is making moonshine in his shell.
He crawls slowly, poisoned with his own success,
dribbling down his shirtfront as he goes.

LUKE KENNARD

SPACESHIPS WITH GUNS BIGGER THAN THE SPACESHIPS THEMSELVES

Elegy for Wizball

Football is a shoot 'em up with one bullet.
Favour the animated waves, beings made of light,

the way they undulate before you kill them:
this is how we would like to encounter the Other,

with kind permission. Why imaginary spaceships
look like contemporary kitchens/bathrooms,

their Dettol cannons. But you, green walnut head,
put us right back in our ill-fitting safari gear.

Everything is elegant on the atomic level:
a wizard with an erection and nobody laughing.

This is a generic 'biker' smashing your head
through the pinball table's glass case

because all costume is costume. Again, the 'biker'
stamping an ice sheet, cracking a crème brûlée.

You are thinking, "Cat in a space ship, cat in a spaceship."
Now he is asking if you enjoyed it. Well?

I think he is a 'sarcastic biker': his tattoos
self-portraits, b&w. This is when they steal all colour

by disappointing or shocking the whole world.
Your car resprayed metallic-No-Longer-Relevant,

jackknifed with the pebble infantry.
May God judge you for what you did in GTA.

Your last words are recorded on a gyroscope
by some idiot who thinks gyroscopes record sound.

PARTIAL INHERITANCE

SONNET FOR WIZKID

If the rodent and the wizard gently sieve
the bugs and paintballs from the right to pay,
Make *Asteroids* the last grand narrative,
What should we build on those foundations, eh?
The coins, piano-soft, fall from the sky,
We juggle televisions on our heads,
A dog sits on the toilet reading why
The riots happened, sleeping with the zeds
Of Tsar czars, czar Tsars, Zsa Zsas and kittens
Rowing backwards to the motherland.
Ignore the clown in stocks: your life depends
On whether anybody tipped the band.
May we suggest you take the bitter pill
with no sophistication but some skill.

SIMON BARRACLOUGH

PIGGLE PEGGLE

I WAS A pig in a poke

little hope

As easy as *stealing acorns*

from a blind pig you wrote

You had me pegged all right

I was pig ignorant then

My thoughts were so bow-legged

they couldn't stop a pig in a passage

You made such a pig of yourself

I thought you'd peg

You said "Pigs get fat

but hogs are slaughtered"

"Put **lipstick on a pig**

it's still a pig"

I retorted

"We're making a pig's ear of this

It's late

C'mon

Pigs in blankets"

EMILY HASLER
OBJECTION!

> Harshly linear.
>
> CRAIG HARRIS REVIEWING *PHOENIX WRIGHT: ACE ATTORNEY*

Before the courtroom
you go to the street

and if you are to go to the street
you must go through the door

that leads to the room
with the door to the street.

It's annoying, but let's not pretend
action isn't made of infinitely smaller actions.

You're here and then you're there,
it's just in life you forget it's all one small step.

And then the next. Slow it down enough
and you'll never cross the room.

Halfway to halfway there
you realise there was a start,

that the things you always say,
the three faces that you wear

are something that became
between beginning and being here.

How easy it is to convince ourselves
that time passes and passes us

when it's us who pass, are passing it:
this bit, this bit, then this.

BEN STAINTON

FINGERS ON PAUSE

Bowser destroying a crate of people
in the castle parlour. It is
a typically green, anthropomorphic
day. Everybody waits – Donkey Kong
painting cityscapes he's never seen,
making butter-yellow sing; Koopa
liquefying dolls, mini-figures, bottlecaps,
fobs, in a sweet bid to assert his personality.
Toad, happy as a mushroom in summer.
The smell of the track exists
in its accessibility only. Mario & Luigi
double-team Peach until noon
as usual. There is a sadness to the bag of pliers
& pipes under the kitchen sink.
There is the sense of pink light falling
through an exposed circuit board. Yoshi
frying eggs on a stolen turtle shell. Bowser
& the empty bottle of gin.

MM

OVERVIEW

I AM THE after-basis; the yellow case no prints are left
On. Obvious limitations – directionally bereft;
A binary-simple compass. Little sun with VFD read-out.
Plagiarism with a capital M.

HARDWARE

Eyes light up via low-voltage mains adaptor. Immutable
Objects effectively fixed, I run on enthusiasm / lack of
Affordable other. At home, battery-less, in compact
Swedish sideboard.

GAMEPLAY

This urge to eat invisible dots; to render colour electric
& real. Real is the guiding tip & risk of actual dissolution
If power-pills unattained. Bite a cherry. Milk the gleaming
Ghosts.

CRITICAL RECEPTION

Weak version my ass. For elementary read essential;
Pure as the day I was born. Shrill beeps / ticking? Always
Deliberate. List product design as 'gorgeous'. Be exhibited.
Have a brochure price of £25.

POSIE RIDER
THE SIMS

In 2005, we gave our navels to mattresses,
shot down & immobile, heads low
my depression was nothing on your detachment.
I have no proof of colours, I'm as real as anything.
They're sandblasting the walls today.
Let's coat this balcony in a dense grey plastic,
let's greet the man
who walks back & forth at floor level,
redistributing space with no respect
for the flying eye of the denizens of multiple stories.
Out of the void & into the screen
we telescope – look at them looking at me
looking at them. I am NOT looking at them
– the man with the hammer
knocking rendering off an exterior I'll never see:
immaterial, commuter, gull!
Impolite voyeur & factotum!
I was born free, & my lover & I
have been established in this burgeoning dwelling.
He is a lonely soul – it means
he doesn't ask how we eat –
his post office account is our crib sheet.
This dense grey film screens out the moon
diffuses night & day, & we are no more bound
to our bodies than the violence of steel on
stone that wakes us.

The coil that we hopelessly decoil
taut & inactive, the bedspread a mile or so
of emerald grass leading to nothing.
Is the glitch the drop of the cigarette,
sheet catching, or the unpeeling of the
body wrap of this expensive building, when
we tear our eyes away to see ourselves
becoming spectacle?
The descending footfall of scales falling,
that's some away date. In the meantime their
little cycle is our cycle, & we live
a thousand days without shifting or ageing
& the hard-hats, they won't intervene.
Sun, begone, moon, reflect not
we are lovers, we have claimed a turgid amnesty
in a blind spot.

DAN SIMPSON

SYMPATHY FOR THE ORANGE GHOST

THERE ARE four ghosts in Pac-Man:
a red one, a pink one, a blue one
and an orange one.

Their names in Japanese are
Akabei, Pinkei, Aosuke and Guzuta:
'Red guy', 'Pink guy', 'Blue guy'
and 'Slow guy'.
Slow orange ghost.

Their characters in Japanese are
Oikake, Machibuse, Kimagure and Otoboke:
'Chaser', 'Ambusher', 'Fickle'
and 'Stupid'.
Stupid, slow orange ghost.

Other names they've been given are:
Urchin, Romp, Stylist
and Crybaby.
Stupid, slow, crybaby orange ghost.

In America they're known as:
Blinky, Pinky, Inky
and Clyde.
Stupid, slow, crybaby orange ghost
who doesn't fit in
because his name doesn't rhyme.

FRANCINE RUBIN

THE WORLD IS TETRIS

Textured geometries fall
from the sky: skyscrapers,
square windows, linoleum tiles,
2 by 4s.

A rectilinear rain forging
right angles everywhere.

Space is always perpendicular,
turning us sideways to the thing
ahead. Movement becomes
an exercise of side-
stepping and avoidance.

We rotate the shapes
as they shower down:

    banquet seating
   on top of
      television set over
 square hole in the wall   near   butcher   blocks

We puzzle-piece
the hail, the speed increasing,
and we scramble to ease
the fettered space:

2 by 4 becomes 4 by 2 next to
skyscraper on its side inside sinkhole   next to   file
                                                        cab-
        Always the obstruction – the   in-
        curbing of limbs with walls.   ets

                We dream in curves,
                where the distance between us is fluid
                like water, where we flow
                outwards.

        Always a division.

        The window before me.

                Outside, things

                tower towards sky.

        We dream in wide-open spaces,   where the distance

        between us is infinite

                and the horizon is empty.

JAMES BROOKES
✿
DIA DE MUERTOS 1998

Boomtown. Later decadence. Our *danse*
macabre is still the Macarena.
Cacao Noir. Aztec Deco. New World Baroque.
The suits polygonic and sharp any script.
Bonemeal feeds the flowers. There is no object
without a witty use we might turn it to.

Sell it to me: an infinite way to chainsmoke;
cracking our knuckles to the open mike;
swigging *Goldschläger* in the airport lobby;
the cackle of perpetual roulette.
In this world so alive with momento mori
no one hears threnody. No sees 'end of an era'.

I'm shipping out in the morning.
Crack a jeroboam over my forehead.
Frieze my puzzled look. Clad my expression in chrome.
I want to pull this moment from my coat
for anyone at any given moment.
Don't tell me you don't really want to do that.

Play it once, for old times' sake. Querida,
love is for the living. Let me have this dance.

HARRY MAN

LINES DERIVED FROM MINECRAFT PLAYER QUERIES

Have you ever spawned like this,
clouds passing through your building
and a blocky dog that will not die
and your wheat disappearing?

Today I checked out the far lands.
What is the best use for gold? Apples?
What do you think the future will be like?
The slow pigs, and 1.6 horses.

Will the air be a fluid like lava?
Will the best trap for a full diamond
be still lagging after a while?
or a cool new skin made just for me?

My skeleton is too fast.
There are so many invisible monsters after death.
I am sick of searching for saddles.
I have a question for you guys,
how rare are villages?

MULTI-PLAYER
✪
STRATEGY POEMS

PLAYERS

Emily Hasler

John Canfield

RULES

In this game, players create a 12-line poem between them, taking it in turns to fill in the lines in any order. At the start of the game, however, each player privately picks a theme and a set of six 'pieces' (words or notions) connected to this theme. They do not share this initially with the other player, but they must use one of these 'pieces' in every line they write. By deploying their pieces, they vie for control over the poem while still collaborating with the other player to make it work as a coherent piece.

Lines are numbered in the order written and themes are revealed at the end, so that the poem can be read both in the order laid out and move by move.

Once the game is finished, players can decide on a title.

EXPOSURE

THE BARELY bitten biscuit, contained in (6)
the very picture book basics of life (4)
cannot be captured by this timid lens. (5)
The aperture is not nearly wide enough (1)
for this black, for this white. (12)
Your eyes are not nearly wide enough (10)
to watch a spectral scene develop, (3)
to see it narrow to a clipped fingernail (8)
as the zoom retracts and the composition dissolves. (9)
Always a surprise, the moon in the still blue sky (2)
like a retina burnt spot that lingers from a flash (7)
but the black is only ever a shutter click away. (11)

EMILY'S THEME: THE MOON
JOHN'S THEME: PHOTOGRAPHY

NOW THEN, VOYAGER

I PACKED my bag, and in it I put just one thing. (3)
Exactingly, I paid the toll. (6)
On days like these, you're skin against skin, (4)
fleeced only with fine hairs that lift against the cold (5)
like a blonde and able crew. My captain, oh my captain. (7)
I waited for the lights to change for days. (2)
How many could see, being so packed in, (8)
how slowly the car moved away, how long to wave? (1)
His shoes wore through, he lined them with plastic bags, sent home (11)
so much stasis, so much lost time. (10)
I boarded with a crowd, he disembarked alone. (12)
Can't you hear me and my boat, knock-knocking at your coastline? (9)

EMILY'S THEME: TRAVELLING
JOHN'S THEME: THE BUS

PLEASE PROVIDE FEEDBACK ON YOUR EXPERIENCE

Would you say that: a) it was painless, or b) (10)

what starts as a soft, low ache becomes (9)

simple really, God/Gods it hurts, just (12)

inevitable really, when immunity fails (3)

but there's something comforting in a fever trap. (5)

Did you know a) before, b) during or (4)

c) after the Apoptosis. Who was it that whispered (11)

did you know that you're bleeding? (1)

They never told you it would hurt. (2)

A change of heart; that ticking liability for this wooden toy. (8)

Your stomach is full of knots, but no more cold feet, child. (6)

It's only a short way down, a fracture at worst, pay it no mind. (7)

Emily's theme: metamorphosis

John's theme: maladies

END OF LEVEL BOSS
HEADSTONE FORTRESS

I.

AND IN ANOTHER short life, my socks were Tintin socks and snowy white. I only stopped running to leap, leaping to run. I fought like a fizzing wasp with zig-zag barb. I had a particular thing for smacking a beat-up ball that could've been a shrunken head, watching it wail. On the clearest of days, with a flagon of cool milk, I would reach base with seconds to spare.

Here lies

s	h	o	r	t	p	a	n	t	s
j	a	c	k	r	a	b	b	i	t
j	e	n	t	p	o	s	e	y	r
n	u	n	k	l	e	e	s	y	i
i	q	i	n	y	t	o	o	a	n
l	n	w	i	n	d	b	a	g	g
m	i	t	t	i	y	b	o	i	b
e	l	t	i	t	h	o	o	l	e
r	e	t	i	b	e	l	k	n	a
g	d	c	n	u	t	c	a	s	n

2.

and in another short life, my head was strapped into a metal bowl, which nodded with me. I sprang with heels flaming. I barrelled on like a loose cart down a gangway, skimming shrapnel. I had a particular thing for pulling the trigger at point blank range, the whinnying kick-back. On the roughest of days, with a chipped spade, I would belt my counterpart senseless.

Here lies

r o c k e t - b o y
h s n u t c a s g a
i i d i s m t b n n
d m p s s i u a o k
i p s p e d c t r e
o l o - i p r t d e
t e l r b e i l i e
p t d e o y a e f l
p o t a t o h e a d
p n p r i v a t e h

3.

and in another short life, my overall bottoms faded to treacle black at the tips of my pins. I lugged an axe and gas canister. I rose like a frogman from the well's skin and roasted ragged ham. I had a particular thing for igniting men made of air, who bawled and slumped to their knees. On the dustiest of days, with a hoarse laugh, I would fire a single flare into the hillside.

Here lies

s	m	o	k	e	y	-	j	o	e
m	u	a	b	o	m	i	n	a	w
n	m	u	t	a	n	t	m	t	h
m	b	m	f	r	e	a	k	i	a
n	l	d	m	s	h	p	m	o	c
p	e	o	n	o	r	o	m	n	k
h	s	p	m	n	a	s	s	i	j
h	d	e	v	i	l	n	m	e	o
h	m	m	m	s	m	n	m	m	b
h	u	d	a	t	h	u	d	d	a

4.

and in another short life, my vest was ballasted – nay, *baubled* – with volatile ampules. I garlanded doorways with explosives. I roared like a waterfall as I closed the distance, crossed the blitzed bridge. I had a particular thing for sending a shower of skittlish sticks down narrow staircases. On the bonniest of days, with a splintered shield, I would carry off many a head.

Here lies

e	y	e	-	p	a	t	c	h	d
y	a	y	r	u	m	m	y	i	r
e	y	e	h	s	u	l	c	r	u
-	r	t	t	i	s	h	l	s	n
h	e	o	t	s	c	o	o	u	k
o	s	c	o	s	o	t	p	t	e
l	s	s	c	o	t	t	s	e	n
e	e	y	a	r	b	o	o	z	e
w	r	e	t	c	h	h	o	u	n
w	d	b	o	t	t	l	e	d	d

5.

and in another short life, my shaved scalp was the prickly cousin to my coalscuttle jaw. I cut perfect bulging sandwiches. I barged like a wild boar through checkpoints, chokepoints, last stands. I had a particular thing for shunting overburdened goods trucks until the rails screamed. On the cloudiest of days, with a giant's kindly hands, I would sow bullets across hectares of hard soil.

Here lies

c	h	u	c	k	w	a	g	o	n
o	o	l	a	r	d	a	s	s	v
r	v	m	b	u	t	t	e	r	p
n	c	o	m	r	a	d	e	m	a
c	f	a	t	i	s	o	i	t	n
a	b	a	l	l	e	l	o	s	c
k	i	v	e	h	s	l	o	b	a
e	v	v	y	b	b	u	h	c	k
s	p	u	t	n	i	f	a	t	e
d	a	r	g	n	i	l	a	t	s

6.

and in another short life, I wore a single JCB-yellow glove, tough as tyre rubber. I surveyed Hell through welding goggles. I worked like a jackhammer to jerryrig all manner of hiccupping, jerking contraptions. I had a particular thing for squatting in a nest of parts while hodge-podge guns raked the dustbowl for squeals. On the busiest of days, with a rust-kissed wrench, I would set the jaws of immaculate traps.

Here lies

b	o	o	k	s	m	a	r	t	s
e	v	g	r	e	a	s	e	o	m
r	e	r	e	c	t	t	y	y	o
e	r	g	h	a	i	a	i	m	n
r	a	h	g	w	n	h	p	a	k
u	l	o	m	h	y	d	p	k	e
o	l	o	y	i	e	r	e	e	y
b	s	y	e	e	g	a	e	r	b
a	h	a	y	t	h	h	d	y	o
l	r	o	s	s	e	f	o	r	p

7.

and in another short life, the knot of my necktie was a blister, a miniature bag of O negative. I always carried an oxygen cylinder. I steered like a mountain goat between rocks ringing with wayward covering fire. I had a particular thing for mending flesh until it sang in all its vigorous impermeability. On the diciest of days, with a needle for every step, I would stitch the ears of the badlands together.

Here lies

d e u t s c h b a g
o z z o a v o t i s
k i e k w o m a n z
t s n t b k o p t v
o p i o o f z i z r
r i c b n u r s e o
z l i e e f p e m n
a l d r s e x r e g
t z e f e s t i n t
n a m e l c a r i m

8.

and in another short life, my knapsack hardly bumped my bootcuts for lack of scurrying. I manned look-out points. I lurked like a beetle at the sharp corner of your eye, a bloody pin-prick. I had a particular thing for gently holing heads through my far-seeing glass, leaving a whistling tunnel. On the dryest of days, with a taut bow and arrow, I would hang a snoop from the barricade by their flak jacket.

Here lies

c	a	m	p	g	r	o	u	n	d
u	g	o	n	a	m	h	s	u	b
p	s	t	i	c	k	q	d	i	u
c	b	e	e	r	u	t	e	a	s
a	a	n	n	a	m	r	a	j	h
k	l	g	t	c	h	i	z	u	c
e	i	t	o	w	u	r	z	d	a
o	e	b	i	l	b	o	i	a	n
r	h	b	a	g	g	i	n	s	t
i	s	w	e	a	s	e	l	o	i

<9.

and in another short life, my suit was as much of a knife as my butterfly knife. I turned into the wind. I arrived like a somnambulist at the enemy gates and played their song. I had a particular thing for jamming electrical devices that whined "Saboteur!" as their hearts failed. On the *rougest* of days, with a damp cigarette, I would betray my closest friend.

Here lies

s	c	o	u	n	d	r	e	l	l
p	n	o	u	h	o	l	a	l	a
o	l	a	a	m	i	s	l	t	s
o	e	s	k	u	n	k	o	u	t
k	r	l	a	e	l	a	u	r	a
s	g	s	t	a	b	b	e	n	b
t	n	n	o	t	u	o	r	c	b
a	o	b	a	c	k	u	u	o	b
b	m	s	t	a	b	b	e	a	e
f	r	e	n	c	h	i	e	t	r

CRETURN OF THE] INTRODUCTION

COMMANDER! I see you've made your way through the whole damned book. Bad news is *cough* I don't think I'll make it. Worse news is ... Commander, I may not have been entirely honest with you. There's no life-sign on my screen and I'm not expecting anyone to get here in time. This is a pre-recorded message. I'm going to set it to play whenever anyone breaches the book. You know, just to start them off on the right foot. I'm sorry – from where I'm sitting, it seems like the only way.

If you're still listening, there's a few more things I thought you should know. *Coin Opera* wasn't the first book of computer game poetry. In 2004, Seth 'Fingers' Flynn Barkan published *Blue Wizard is About to Die*, describing the contents as 'prose, poems and emoto-versatronic expressionist pieces about video games'. In 2012, Gregory Sherl's *The Oregon Trail is the Oregon Trail* appeared, a sequence of poems whose narrator appears to be trapped within *The Oregon Trail*, endlessly reliving the events of the game. There's an argument for game poetry as an emergent genre – a number of the poems selected for this anthology had already been published, and others we commissioned have since gone on to slot neatly into the poets' individual oeuvres.

At the same time, independent game developers are setting out in increasing numbers to explore the possibilties for poetry within gaming. *Silent Conversation* by Gregory Weir reproduces and rearranges classical poems (as well as short stories) as game levels that the player, represented as an I-beam cursor, must navigate, avoiding the 'echoes' of 'powerful' words that are marked in red. Players are then graded according to how many of the words they have physically touched.

Ian Bogost's *A Slow Year* is an electronic chapbook of four poem-games, one for each season, embracing "maximum expressive constraint and representational condensation" and aspiring toward "a video game version of Imagism". Bogost coded the games for an ancient system, the Atari, specifically because of the system's lower-end technical capabilities. He is one of those developers I mentioned earlier who is aware of the value in formal restrictions and the role they have in creating poetry. Of *A Slow Year*, he writes:

> As games, these rely on the procedural representation of an idea that the player manipulates. As poetry, they rely on the condensation of symbols and concepts rather than the clarification of specific experiences.

Beyond these games-as-poems and the examples in this book of poems-as-games, there surely lies the possibility of the hybrid, a form which is both game and poem at once. While this is rather exciting, it should not be mistaken for an ultimate goal; the entire spectrum of possible interactions between the two mediums is fit for further exploration. There's clearly scope for games to enhance, democratise or subvert the experience of poetry for future generations, rescuing it from the fringes to which it has temporarily retreated. Similarly, poetry offers the chance to enrich and prolong the life of games by suggesting new ways to experience and interpret them, by making something *of* them. The vast remaining potential in each medium is multiplied further when the two are permitted to invade each other's space, so to speak.

And with that *cough, cough* my goose is cooked. *Cough*

> *Player 'Jon Stone' has perished.*

INDEX BY GAME TITLE

Altered Beast 78

Bioshock 96–97

Braid 88

Bride of Pinbot 111

Daley Thompson's Supertest 40–42

Donkey Kong 79

Doomdark's Revenge 98-99

Dragon's Lair 78–79

Elder Scrolls V: Skyrim 69

Final Fantasy IV 64–66

Final Fantasy VII 86–87

Fist of the North Star 19

Gauntlet (series) 82–85

God of War (series) 34–35

Golden Axe 44, 50–51

Grim Fandango 136

Guilty Gear Accent Core Plus 54–55

ICO 92–93

The King of Fighters 2000 51–52

The Legend of Zelda: Twilight Princess 72–73

The Legend of Zelda: Ocarina of Time 71

The Legend of Zelda: Link's Awakening 70

Lemmings 116–117

Manic Miner 89

Mario Kart 128

Metal Slug (series) 52–54

Metroid 68

Minecraft 137

Mortal Kombat (series) 43

Pac-Man 127, 132–133

Peggle 125

Pinball Dreams 114–115

Planescape: Torment 104–110

Pokemon (series) 112

Phoenix Wright: Ace Attorney 126–127

Prince of Persia 76

Okami 75

Resident Evil (series) 38–39

Robot Unicorn Attack 74

Sabre Wulf 90

Samurai Shodown (series) 24–31

Samorost 120–121

Shadow of the Colossus 32–33

The Sims 130–131

Snake 118

Soldier of Fortune 42

Sonic the Hedgehog (series) 77

Street Fighter II 21-23, 48–49

Streets of Rage 37

Super Mario Bros 67

Target: Renegade 20

Team Fortress 2 142–150

Tekken (series) 36

Terraria 94–95

Tetris 132–133

Tomb Raider 58–63

Valhalla 91

Wizball 122–123

Wizkid 124

Zookeeper 119

NOTES & CHEATS

pp.22-29, *How Weak You Are* – The form is pseudo-senryu, while the syntax mimics the botched translations (or 'Engrish') of the Samurai Shodown game series. Senryu are a Japanese form similar to haiku but not requiring a *kigo* (season word), tending instead to be witty and observational.

pp.34, *Tekken Love Poem* – In fighting games like *Tekken*, special moves are performed through sequences of button presses. The symbols used in this poem represent instructions on which buttons to press on a Playstation-type controller.

pp.35, *Side Scroller* – Narrative-based games of the 16-bit era generally did not grant the option to save your progress and reload after defeat. For every session, the player was instead granted a limited number of 'lives' and 'continues' – chances to return from the dead. Each 'continue' was worth about three 'lives'.

pp.41, *Pit Boss* – Shao Kahn is the final boss in most *Mortal Kombat* games, the demonic ruler of a parallel dimension called Outworld.

pp.42, *Golden Axe* – Death Adder is the name of the game's antagonist.

pp.63, *Caligula as a Character in Final Fantasy* – 'You spoony bard!' is an infamous line from the original English translation of *Final Fantasy IV*.

pp.66, *That Metroid Guy Is A Lady* – The original *Metroid* is notable for being one of the first computer games to feature a female protagonist, a fact which is only revealed at the completion of the game, when she removes her space helmet.

pp.75, *Sonic Senryu* – See explanation of senryu above.

pp.84, *The October Revolution and a Golden Chocobo* – In *Final Fantasy VII*, chocobo were giant birds that the player could catch, use as mounts and then breed. The hardest (and most practically useful) variant to breed was the golden chocobo. The PS1 was the first Playstation console.

pp.86, *Past Simple* – Indie game *Braid* allowed the player to manipulate the passage of time to complete certain tasks, even reversing it until they return to the very beginning of the level.

pp.100, *Cento for a Nameless One* – The Nameless One is the protagonist/player character in *Planescape: Torment*, an immortal amnesiac whose past lives continue to haunt him. A cento is a poem composed entirely out of lines from other poems. Jon adds: "To credit the sources of all the lines here would somewhat defeat the object of the exercise. The poem envisages readers getting a sense of déjà vu from encountering lines they may have read in the past, but not necessarily being able to identify them."

pp.136, *Headstone Fortress* – The typical lifespan of a player in a team-based competitive first person shooter like *Team Fortress 2* is but a few minutes. After they die, they have the option to come back as another character, cycling through nine classes in total.

CREDITS

E. Kristin Anderson grew up in Westbrook, Maine, and is a graduate of Connecticut College. She has a fancy diploma that says "BA in Classics", which makes her sound smart but has not helped her get any jobs in Ancient Rome. Ms. Anderson is the co-editor of the anthology *Dear Teen Me*, and her poetry has been published worldwide in many magazines, as well as in the YA sci-fi anthology *Futuredaze*, forthcoming from Underwords. She now lives in Austin, Texas, where she is an assistant YA and children's editor at *Hunger Mountain*. **ekristinanderson.com** and **metremaids.com**

Simon Barraclough is the author of *Los Alamos Mon Amour* (Salt Publishing, 2008), *Bonjour Tetris* (Penned in the Margins, 2010) and *Neptune Blue* (Salt Publishing, 2011). He is the editor of *Psycho Poetica* (Sidekick Books, 2012).

James Brookes was born in 1986 and grew up in rural Sussex. He received an Eric Gregory Award in 2009 and a Hawthornden International Writer's Fellowship in 2011. He has published a pamphlet, *The English Sweats*, with Pighog Press and a full collection, *Sins of the Leopard* (Salt Publishing, 2012).

Phil Brown was born in London in 1987. He is a high school English teacher and poetry editor for the website Silkworms Ink. His first collection, *Il Avilit*, was released with Nine Arches Press in 2011. A pamphlet, *Oh*, was released by Holdfire Press in 2012.

Sam Buchan-Watts graduated from Goldsmiths College in 2010. He is co-editor of the *Clinic* anthologies. Sam works for the literary magazine *Five Dials* and the independent bookshop John Sandoe's.

www.clinicpresents.com and **www.fivedials.com**

Niall Campbell is originally from the Western Isles of Scotland. He studied English Literature at Glasgow University, and in 2009 went on to complete an MLitt in Creative Writing at the University of St Andrews. In 2011 he received an Eric Gregory Award and a Robert Louis Stevenson Fellowship. His first pamphlet, *After the Creel Fleet*, was released by Happenstance Press in 2012.

John Canfield grew up in Cornwall and now lives and writes in London. He trained as an actor, but due to a clerical misunderstanding works as an accounts administrator.

@JohnCanfield_

Chelsea Cargill lives in Edinburgh. She has had poetry published in *The Delinquent* and a story about a talking ventriloquist dummy bear in a New Voices Press anthology. She co-runs the Edinburgh Antisocial Writers Club.

chelseacargill.wordpress.com

Kayo Chingonyi's first pamphlet of poems, *Some Bright Elegance*, is out now from Salt Publishing. His website is **kchingonyi.wordpress.com**.

John Clegg's work has been included in the *Salt Book of Younger Poets* and *The Best British Poetry 2012* (both Salt Publishing). His first collection, *Antler*, was also published by Salt in 2012.

Isobel Dixon's collections *The Tempest Prognosticator* and *A Fold in the Map* are published by Salt. Her work is featured in *Birdbook I: Towns, Parks, Gardens and Woodland* and *Psycho Poetica* (both Sidekick Books), Penguin's *Poems for Love* and Salt's *The Best British Poetry 2011*. She co-wrote and performed *The Debris Field* (Sidekick Books, 2013). **isobeldixon.com**

Joe Dunthorne can sing the loading music from *The Last Ninja*. **joedunthorne.com**

In the old days, **David Floyd** wrote poetry. Now he mainly writes about social enterprise at **beanbagsandbullshit.com**.

S. J. Fowler has published four collections of poetry and 12 chapbooks, and has featured in around 100 magazines. His work has been commissioned by Tate Britain, the London Sinfonietta and *Mercy*. He runs the *Maintenant* reading and interview series, and is the poetry editor for the magazines *3am* and *VLAK*, and *Lyrikline* in the UK. A former *Championship Manager* addict and professional mixed martial artist, he currently works in the British Museum. See **sjfowlerpoetry.com** or **blutkitt.blogspot.com**.

Charlotte Geater lives in East London, is studying for an MA at the University of Kent, and works in publishing. She has been published in *The Salt Book of Younger Poets* and *The Rialto*. **@tambourine**.

Matt Haigh lives in Cardiff, in near-perpetual nostalgia for the golden years of the N64 and Dreamcast. Some of his poems have appeared in *Poetry London*, *Magma*, *The Guardian* and *Fuselit*. His blog can be found at **matthewhaighpoetry.com**.

 **Cliff Hammett** writes, draws, and tinkers with electronic and other media. He is a member of the Open Systems Association, which explores the agency of systems, processes and objects through errant experimentation, and he contributes to the arts and technologies journal *Flee Immediately*.

Emily Hasler was born in Felixstowe, Suffolk, studied at the University of Warwick and now co-runs the *Broadcast* events series. In 2009 she came second in the Edwin Morgan International Poetry Competition. Her poems have appeared in *The Rialto, Poetry Salzburg* and *The Best British Poetry 2011*. Her debut pamphlet, *Natural Histories*, was published by Salt in 2011. Her game of choice is *Minesweeper*.

 **Holly Hopkins** lives and works in London. Her poems have been published in *Poetry Review*, *The Rialto*, *The North* and *Magma*. She has also been anthologised in *Birdbook I* (Sidekick Books), *The Captain's Tower* (Seren Books), *Herbarium* (Capsule Press), *Lung Jazz: Young British Poets for Oxfam* (Cinnamon Press) and *Dear World & Everyone In It: New Poetry In the UK* (Bloodaxe Books, due 2013). Holly received an Eric Gregory Award in 2011. **hollyhopkins.co.uk**

Kirsten Irving enjoys watching *Zool* being played, but is too lazy to do much beyond turning the cardboard wheel to find the password needed to start the game. Her first collection, *Never Never Never Come Back*, is available from Salt Publishing. **@KoftheTriffids**

Luke Kennard is a writer and award-winning poet. His pamphlet, *The Necropolis Boat*, was commended by the Poetry Book Society, and his science fiction novella, *Holophin*, is available from Penned in the Margins. He blogs at **planetshapedhorse.blogspot.com** and lectures at the University of Birmingham.

Melissa Lee-Houghton's first collection, *A Body Made of You*, is published by Penned in the Margins. Her poetry and short fiction have appeared widely in magazines, most recently in *Tears in the Fence* and *Poetry Salzburg Review*. She is a contributor to *The Silent History,* a global project that involves reading narratives on iPhones at specific locations as part of a wider literary experience. **melissaleehoughton.wordpress.com**

Harry Man works as a digital editor in South London. His poetry has appeared in *Poems in the Waiting Room*, *New Welsh Review*, *Astronaut* and *Fuselit*, among other places. He is a member of Malika Booker's Poetry Kitchen. **manmadebooks.co.uk**

Harriet Moore is from South London and recently graduated from UCL with a BA in English Literature. She has been published in *Magma* and *Clinic* and her poems feature in *The Salt Book of Younger Poets* and *The Best British Poetry 2012*. She works for a literary agent and co-edits an arts blog.

Gabrielle Nolan loves poems. She would probably love you too, given an opportunity and a nice cup of tea with milk and honey.

Abigail Parry lives in London, and is currently studying towards a PhD in poetics. Her poems have been published in various magazines, including *Poetry London*, *The Rialto*, *Ambit* and *Magma*, and in the anthologies *The Best British Poetry 2011*, *Lung Jazz* and *Clinic II*. She received an Eric Gregory Award in 2010.

Nathan Penlington is a writer, performer and obsessive. He has performed his work in venues as diverse as Tate Modern, Oxford Literary Festival and Chicago's Drinking & Writing Festival, and has been broadcast on BBC Radio 1, 3 and 4. In 2013, he took *Choose Your Own Documentary*, a show based around adventure gamebooks, to the Edinburgh Fringe Festival. **nathanpenlington.com**

Kate Potts lives and works in London. Her pamphlet, *Whichever Music* (tall-lighthouse, 2008) was a Poetry Book Society Choice in 2008 and was shortlisted for a Michael Marks Award. *Pure Hustle* (Bloodaxe Books, 2011) is her first book-length collection.

Samuel Prince was born in 1980 and brought up in West Yorkshire and Norfolk. He studied at the University of Manchester and now lives and works in London. Poems of his can be found in various online and print journals as well as in Sidekick Books' *Birdbook II*.

Posie Rider is all I. A post-riot suffragette with a telepathic cat, she can be found grimacing at the yummy mummies of Islington most weekdays over a vanilla spiced latte. When not agitating for full communism and real

feminism, she is writing, which is in effect, her act. Her copious books include *City Break Weekend Songs* (Critical Documents, 2011) and *tristanundisolde* (Arthur Shilling Press, 2009 – SOLD OUT, but she could photocopy you one if you like). Poems implicate themselves globally. Readings occur spontaneously. When she grows up she wants to live on a farm. She is currently working on her first novel. Contact her at **posierider@gmail.com**.

 **Francine Rubin** is the author of the chapbook *Geometries* (Finishing Line Press, 2012). Her poems have also appeared in *Anomalous Press, Fuselit, Fringe Magazine, Ozone Park Journal,* and *Rougarou,* among others. She works as the associate director of the Learning Center at SUNY Purchase College, where she also teaches writing. **francinerubin.tumblr.com**

Charlotte Runcie is a former Foyle Young Poet of the Year and winner of the Christopher Tower Poetry Prize. A pamphlet of her poems, *seventeen horse skeletons*, is published by tall-lighthouse, and she features in *The Salt Book of Younger Poets*. She lives in Edinburgh. Follow **@charlotteruncie** on Twitter.

 **Dan Simpson** is a spoken word poet and compère, poetry projects and event organiser, workshop facilitator and writer. He creates pioneering work with crowdsourced and outdoor poetry, and is the host of The Word House in London. He has performed for the BBC and his poetry has featured on London Underground. **dansimpsonpoet.co.uk**

Ben Stainton's poems appear in *The Rialto, Magma* and *Stop Sharpening Your Knives 4* and *5*, as well as in the anthologies *Lung Jazz* and the forthcoming *Dear World & Everyone In It* (Bloodaxe Books, 2013). He occasionally reviews for *Eyewear*.

Jon Stone is one of the editors of Sidekick Books. He was awarded an Eric Gregory Award in 2012 and his book, *School of Forgery* (Salt Publishing, 2012), was a Poetry Book Society summer recommendation. **www.gojonstonego.com**

Mike Stone – When Jon failed to return from the first *Coin Opera* and rumour of Dr. F's survival reached his clan, they immediately sent another assassin to complete the task. This new warrior is actually Jon's younger brother. He enters armed with a blunt pencil and a brush choked with paint. **www.mikescribbles.com**

Ross Sutherland was born in Edinburgh in 1979. An ex-lecturer in Electronic Literature at Liverpool John Moores University, he now works as a poet and tutor. His collections include *Things To Do Before You Leave Town*, *Hyakuretsu Kyaku*, *Twelve Nudes* and *Emergency Window* (all published by Penned in the Margins). **www.rosssutherland.co.uk**.

Claire Trevien's pamphlet, *Low-Tide Lottery*, was published by Salt in 2011, and her first collection, *The Shipwrecked House*, was published by Penned in the Margins in 2013. She edits Sabotage Reviews, which can be found at **sabotagereviews.com**.

Richard Watt lives in Angus, Scotland, and divides his time between being a new father, sitting in courtrooms and getting shouted at by farmers. His first pamphlet, *The Golem*, was published by Holdfire Press in 2012.

Aliya Whiteley's first two novels were published by Macmillan, and *Witchcraft in the Harem*, a collection of her speculative short fiction, was published by Dog Horn

Publishing in 2013. Her writing has appeared in places as diverse as *The Guardian*, *McSweeney's*, *Strange Horizons*, *Lonely Planet*, *The Drabblecast* and *Per Contra*. **aliyawhiteley.wordpress.com**.

Ben Wilkinson was shortlisted for the inaugural Picador Poetry Prize. *The Sparks* was published by tall-lighthouse in 2008; he is working towards a first collection, *First Glance*.

Chrissy Williams lives in London and works at the Poetry Library. She has been published in various magazines and anthologies, including *The Rialto*, *Poetry Review*, *SSYK*, *Horizon Review*, *Fuselit*, *Adventures in Form* (Penned in the Margins, 2012) and *The Best British Poetry 2011*. Her first pamphlet, *The Jam Trap*, a collaboration with comic book artists, was published in 2012 by Soaring Penguin.